Eric Kayser's

SWEET AND SAVORY TARTS

Translated from the French by Carmella Abramowitz-Moreau
Art direction: Studio de création Flammarion
Typesetting: Claude-Olivier Four
Copyediting: Penny Isaac
Proofreading: Philippa Hurd

Distributed in North America by Rizzoli International Publications, Inc.

Originally published in French as *Les Tartes d'Eric Kayser* © 2006 Flammarion, SA

English-language edition © 2007 Flammarion, SA

07 08 09 3 2 1
ISBN 10: 2-0803-0556-5
ISBN 13: 978-2-0803-0556-5
Dépôt légal: 04/2007

www.editions.flammarion.com

Printed in Singapore by Tien Wah Press

Eric Kayser

Photographs by Christian Larit

Eric Kayser's
SWEET AND SAVORY TARTS

Flammarion

Contents

I make tarts the way
a bread baker makes them

...because I'm a bread baker at heart. For me, every step of the process comes naturally: touching the dough, kneading it, lining a pan, and filling it with generous spoonfuls of creamy batters that I spread over with fruit or vegetables. There is nothing I find more satisfying than waiting near the oven with the expectation of sharing this happiness with others. It's a simple pleasure, like good bread.

I was lucky to be born into a family of bakers. I would wake up to the sweet smells of croissants baking, and fall asleep near the comforting warmth of my father's oven. As a small boy in Lure, in the Franche-Comté region of eastern France, I loved to scatter the first blueberries of the season on delicate puff pastry. Concentrating hard, I would arrange slices of ripe apples on freshly prepared dough, watch as the tarts disappeared into the oven, and wait eagerly for them to reappear, great and gleaming, in our store.

This is where my vocation began, as I scrubbed my father's trays, breathing in the wholesome aroma of the flour, in tune with the flavors of each season. From the age of seven, I knew that I would make the staff of life: good bread.

The tarts came later. They followed on naturally from the way I was already working: something delicious on top of an appetizing, crisp crust. I like tarts that can be described as "rustic." You can see straightaway what they're all about; there's nothing intricate to them. Biting into tarts like this, with their juicy fruit and golden crust, is a simple, basic pleasure. I'd like you to share my joy in making them, and hope you agree that they can be food for the soul. When your friends and family dig in, you'll prove to them that "tarts" and "tenderness" have more in common than just their first letter.

ERIC KAYSER

My Favorite Pastries

There's no pleasure more down-to-earth than making pastry crusts—from light, crumbly shortbread to airy, delicate, melt-in-your-mouth puff pastry, to the dough for brioche that's moist and smooth.

Some Helpful Hints

* The pastry recipes that follow make sufficient quantities for three 9 ½-inch (24-cm) square tarts or three 10-inch (26-cm) round tarts.
  Divide the dough into three equal parts, one to use immediately. Cover the other two in plastic wrap and freeze for future use.

* To defrost, place the frozen dough in the refrigerator the day before you need it to thaw slowly. Take it out from the refrigerator 15 minutes before using it.

* You can buy products such as tapenade (green and black olive paste, a specialty from the south of France), goat's-milk cheese, and crème fraîche at finer grocery stores and wholefood supermarkets. If you can't find crème fraîche, use heavy cream. Pistachio paste can be bought online. Chocolate should have a minimum of 55 percent cacao, unless milk or white chocolate is called for. Try farmers' markets for wild mushrooms and other fresh produce.

SHORTBREAD PASTRY

Preparation time: 10 minutes
Refrigeration time: overnight
To make three 9 ½-inch (24-cm)
square tarts or three 10-inch
(26-cm) round tarts.

Ingredients

1 ⅓ cup (300 g) unsalted butter, softened
⅓ cup (60 g) granulated sugar
1 cup (125 g) confectioners' sugar
1 teaspoon (5 g) salt
2 eggs
1 ¼ lb or 6 ¼ cups (560 g) cake flour

↻ A day ahead

In the mixing bowl of a food processor, cream the butter.
Mix in the granulated sugar, the confectioners' sugar, and the salt.

Add the eggs, one by one. Pour in the flour and mix thoroughly.

Form the dough into a ball, cover with plastic wrap, and refrigerate overnight.

Quince Tart
with Mead
⟶ p. 102

White Chocolate
and Raspberry
Tart
⟶ p. 142

Fig and Pecan Tart
⟶ p. 156

11

ALMOND SHORTBREAD PASTRY

Preparation time: 10 minutes
Refrigeration time: overnight
To make 3 tarts, 9 ½ inches (24 cm)
square or 10 inches (26 cm) round.

Ingredients

1 ⅓ cups (300 g) unsalted butter, softened
⅓ cup (60 g) granulated sugar
1 cup (125 g) confectioners' sugar
¾ cup (60 g) ground almonds
1 teaspoon (5 g) salt
2 eggs
5 ½ cups (500 g) cake flour

A day ahead

In a food-processor bowl, cream the butter.

Mix in the granulated sugar, the confectioners' sugar, the ground almonds, and the salt.

Add the eggs one by one, beating continuously.

Pour in the flour and mix thoroughly.

Form the dough into a ball, cover in plastic wrap, and refrigerate overnight.

Pear and
Grapefruit Tart
⟶ p. 74

Damson
Plum Tart
⟶ p. 82

Chocolate
Hazelnut Tart
⟶ p. 126

BRETON SHORTBREAD PASTRY

Preparation time: 10 minutes
Refrigeration time: overnight
To make 3 tarts, 9 ½ inches (24 cm)
square or 10 inches (26 cm) round.

Ingredients

¾ cup (180 g) unsalted butter, softened
¾ cup plus 1 tablespoon (160 g) granulated sugar
1 teaspoon (5 g) salt
2 eggs
2 ⅔ cups (240 g) cake flour
1 tablespoon (12 g) baking powder

A day ahead

In the mixing bowl of a food processor, cream the butter.

Add the sugar and the salt. Mix through.

Incorporate the eggs, one by one, mixing constantly.
Pour in the flour and the baking powder. Mix thoroughly.

Form a ball with the dough, cover in plastic wrap, and refrigerate overnight.

Breton Shortbread
with Wild
Strawberries
⟶ p. 113

CHOCOLATE SHORTBREAD PASTRY

Preparation: 10 minutes
Refrigeration: overnight
To make 3 tarts, 9 ½ inches (24 cm)
square or 10 inches (26 cm) round.

Ingredients

1 cup (250 g) unsalted butter, softened
1 cup plus 2 tablespoons (150 g)
confectioners' sugar
½ cup (50 g) ground hazelnuts
2 level teaspoons (5 g) ground cinnamon
2 eggs
4 ½ cups (400 g) cake flour
2 ½ teaspoons (10 g) baking powder
1 ½ tablespoons (10 g) cocoa powder

A day ahead

In the mixing bowl of a food processor, cream the butter.

Add the confectioners' sugar, the ground hazelnuts, and the cinnamon, and mix together.

Add the eggs, one by one, mixing constantly.

Sift in the flour, the baking powder, and the cocoa powder, and mix well.

Form a ball with the dough, cover in plastic wrap, and chill overnight.

Bittersweet
Chocolate Tart
→ p. 132

Chocolate
Trio
→ p. 136

Chestnut Tart
→ p. 152

PUFF PASTRY

Preparation time: 20 minutes
Can be prepared a day ahead
Resting time: 4 hours
To make 3 tarts, 9 ½ inches (24 cm)
square or 10 inches (26 cm) round.

Ingredients

2 cups (480 g) unsalted butter
¾ cup (200 ml) tap water (not too cold)
5 ½ cups (500 g) cake flour
2 teaspoons (10 g) salt

↻ A day ahead

Melt ½ cup (100 g) of the butter. In the mixing bowl of a food processor, mix the flour, the melted butter, ¾ cup tap water until all ingredients are thoroughly blended. Set aside to rest for 1 hour at room temperature. (This may be prepared a day ahead.)

Apple
and Raisin Tart
→ p. 121

1. Slightly soften the remaining 1 ½ cups butter. Roll the dough out with a rolling pin into a neat rectangle. Place the butter in the center of this rectangle.

2. Fold each flap of the dough over the butter to cover it completely. Roll out the dough to a strip ¼ inch (6 mm) thick.

3. Fold the dough over itself 3 times. Roll out again to a thickness of ¼ inch (6 mm). Fold over again 3 times.

4. Leave the dough to rest for 1 hour at room temperature.

5. Repeat the operation twice, leaving the dough to rest for 1 hour each time.

6. Roll the dough into a rectangle on a worktop. Cover in plastic wrap and refrigerate.

PISTACHIO DACQUOISE PASTRY

Preparation: 15 minutes
Baking time: 20 minutes
To make 3 tarts, 9 ½ inches (24 cm)
square or 10 inches (26 cm) round.

_____

Ingredients

6 egg whites
1 ¼ cups (160 g) confectioners' sugar
1 oz (24 g) pistachio paste
1 ⅔ cups (140 g) ground almonds
⅓ cup (60 g) superfine sugar
1 oz (32 g) unsalted pistachios, ground
Butter for the mold

✕ This can't be frozen, so plan to make it the day you need it

Beat the egg whites stiffly with the confectioners' sugar. Add 1 tablespoon of beaten egg whites to the pistachio paste to soften it, and then incorporate the paste into the rest of the egg whites.

Mix together the ground almonds, the superfine sugar, and the ground unsalted pistachios. Fold these ingredients gently into the beaten egg whites.

Butter a mold and spoon the pastry into it. Bake for 20 minutes at 325°F (160°C). Allow to cool before garnishing.

Strawberries
on Pistachio
Dacquoise
—→ p. 88

VIENNOISE PASTRY

Preparation time: 20 minutes
Resting time: 1 hour 15 minutes
Baking time: 15 minutes
To make 3 tarts, 9 ½ inches (24 cm)
square or 10 inches (26 cm) round.

_____

Ingredients

5 ½ cups (500 g) cake flour or 5 cups
(500 g) all-purpose flour
2 teaspoons (11 g) salt
⅓ cup (70 g) superfine sugar
7 tablespoons (50 g) powdered milk
2 ½ teaspoons (15 g) yeast
⅔ cup (150 g) unsalted butter, softened
1 cup (250 ml) tap water
Optional: dried fruit, spices, or seeds

Put the flour, the salt, the sugar, the powdered milk, the yeast, and the butter into the mixing bowl of a food processor. Add 1 cup (250 ml) of water and knead for 15 minutes. Then add the dried fruit, spices, or seeds if using.

Leave to rise for 15 minutes at room temperature.

Roll out the dough to about 1-inch (2.5-cm) thickness and leave to rise again for 1 hour at room temperature. Bake for 15 minutes at 350°F (180°C).

CROISSANT PASTRY

Preparation time: 30–60 minutes
Refrigeration time: 1 hour
Resting time: 1 hour
To make 4 tarts, 9 ½ inches (24 cm)
square or 10 inches (26 cm) round,
or 20 croissants.

Ingredients

3 ⅓ cups (300 g) cake flour
2 ½ cups (250 g) all-purpose flour
3 teaspoons (17 g) yeast
⅓ cup (70 g) superfine sugar
1 egg
1 cup (225 g) unsalted butter, softened
2 teaspoons (10 g) salt
¾ cup (200 ml) water

In the mixing bowl of a food processor, mix the two flours with the yeast, the sugar, the egg, ¾ cup (200 ml) water, 1 ½ tablespoons softened butter, and the salt. Knead for 10 minutes.

Form a ball with the dough, cover in plastic wrap, and chill for 1 hour.
Flatten out the dough with a rolling pin to about 1 inch (2.5 cm).

Place the remaining butter in the center and fold over the dough to cover it. Roll out again in a rectangle, approximately 24 inches long (60–70 cm) long. Fold the dough in three. Repeat the process twice.

Leave the dough to rest for 1 hour at room temperature. Cut off the quantity you will need and roll it out according to what you're planning to make. Cover the rest with plastic wrap and refrigerate it.

Mango Upside-
Down Cake
→ p. 98

17

BRIOCHE PASTRY

Preparation time: 20 minutes
Refrigeration time: 12 hours
To make 3 tarts, 9 ½ inches (24 cm)
square or 10 inches (26 cm) round.

🕐 A day ahead

Ingredients

5 ½ cups (500 g) cake flour
6 eggs
¼ cup (50 g) superfine sugar
2 teaspoons (10 g) salt
1 tablespoon (20 g) yeast
1 ½ cups (350 g) unsalted butter,
softened

Pink Caramelized
Almond Tart
→ p. 155

1. Pour the flour into a mixing bowl or onto a worktop.

2. Lightly beat the eggs. Make a well in the flour and pour them in.

3. Add the sugar, the salt, and the yeast. . .

4. . . . and incorporate the softened butter.

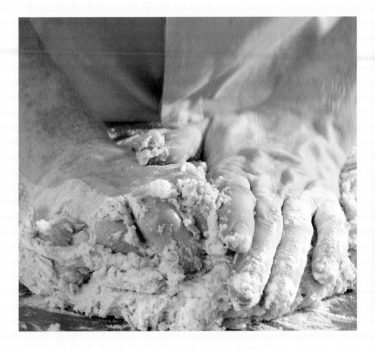

5. Knead for 15 minutes.

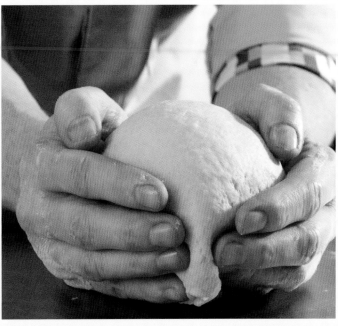

6. Form the dough into a ball, cover with plastic wrap, and chill overnight.

SAVORY PÂTE BRISÉE (PIE PASTRY)

Preparation time: 15 minutes
Refrigeration time: 30 minutes
Resting time: 15 minutes
To make one 9 ½ inches (24 cm)
square or one 10 inches
(26 cm) round.

Ingredients

2 ⅓ cups (210 g) flour, and a little extra
for the worktop
1 teaspoon (5 g) salt
½ cup (100 g) unsalted butter, softened
and diced
¼ cup (65 ml) tap water

Sift the flour together with the salt into a mixing bowl through a fine sieve. Make a well in the center of the flour and add the diced butter. Mix it together by hand.

Again, use your fingers to make a well in the mixture. Pour in ¼-cup (65-ml) water. Knead the dough quickly with your fingertips until it forms a firm ball.

Lightly sprinkle a little flour on the working surface and flatten the dough with the palm of your hand. Reshape it into a ball. Repeat the process once more. Cover the ball of dough in plastic wrap.

Chill it for approximately 30 minutes, then leave it to rest for about 15 minutes at room temperature. Lightly dust a rolling pin with flour and roll out the dough. Line the baking pan.

Return it to the refrigerator and take it out 15 minutes before baking.

Smoked Trout
and Fennel Tart
→ p. 32

Chicken,
Eggplant, and
Coconut Milk Tart
→ p. 38

Artichoke,
Tapenade, and
Parmesan Quiche
→ p. 66

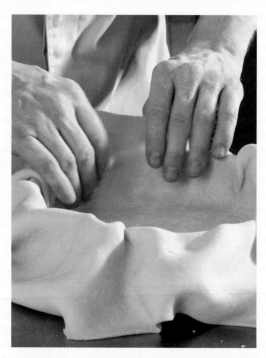

FOUGASSE PASTRY

Preparation time: 20 minutes
Resting time: 1 hour
To make 3 tarts, 9 ½ inches (24 cm)
square or 10 inches (26 cm) round.

Ingredients

5 ½ cups (500 g) cake flour
1 cup (250 ml) olive oil
2 ¼ teaspoons (12 g) salt
2 teaspoons (10 g) yeast
2 tablespoons (10 g) Herbes de Provence
1 ½ teaspoons (5 g) granulated sugar
3 ½ (50 ml) tablespoons tap water

Place all the ingredients in the mixing bowl of a food processor.
Knead for 10 minutes.

Line a baking tray with parchment or waxed paper and roll out the dough to
a thickness of just under 1 inch. Allow to rise for 1 hour at room temperature.

Marinated
Salmon and
Mozzarella Tart
→ p. 54

Oyster
Mushroom
and Bacon
Bit Quiche
→ p. 62

Scallop
and Zucchini Tart
→ p. 70

PRE-BAKING

Pre-baking, also known as "baking blind," means baking the shell before you garnish it.

Lightly prick the shell all over using a fork. Place a sheet of parchment or waxed paper over the shell.

Cover the paper evenly with dried pulses (for example, beans or lentils) so that the pastry does not rise.

Bake for 20 minutes in an oven preheated to 350°F (180°C).

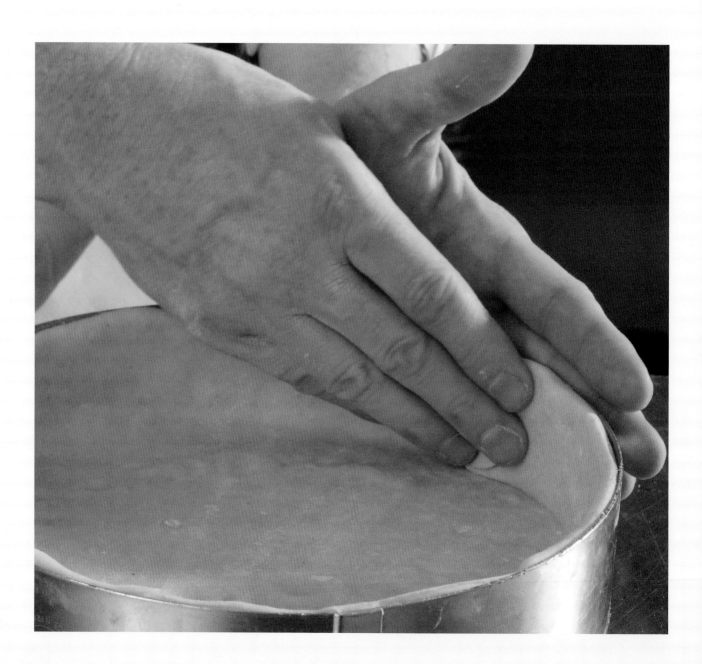

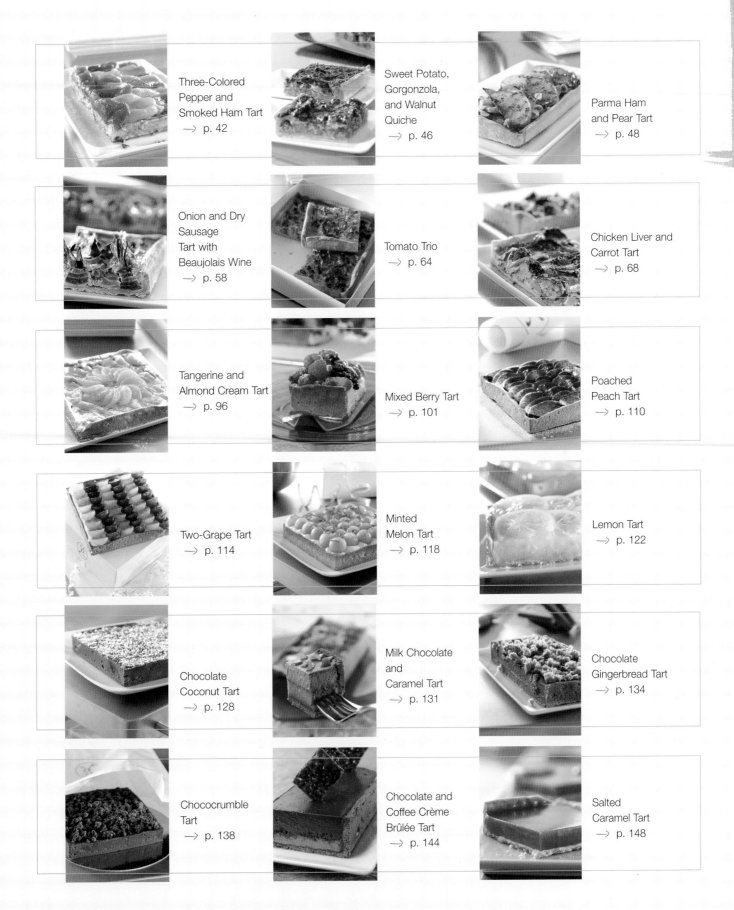

ERIC KAYSER

My Secrets

There's only one real secret to making good tarts, and that is time. Look after the pastry you make: let it breath; let it relax. That's why it is best to prepare your crust a day ahead.

If you want your tart to taste delicious and look wonderful, you must make your pastry with care. That's the part that will elicit cries of, "Oh, that tart looks delicious!" This means you must concentrate and work meticulously—but that's not complicated.

1. Selecting a good flour

This is an essential ingredient. It's hard to find the flours that professionals use, but try to use cake flour, without additives or raising agents, to make sweet pastries. For doughs that rise (brioche, fougasse, viennoise, and croissant)—which all need more elasticity—all-purpose flour, which is denser, is preferable.

2. Choosing the freshest, best-quality ingredients

You need freshly laid eggs, and you should try to find the large ones. Buy the best-quality butter, preferably unsalted. The type of sugar varies with the recipes—superfine sugar, brown sugar, confectioners' sugar, and so on. The finer it is, the more quickly it will dissolve, meaning you won't need to overwork your pastries and batters. Only one choice of milk is possible: whole milk. Use fresh whipping cream for the sweet tarts, and thick, heavy cream for the savory quiches to give them a tang.

Buy fresh seasonal fruit and vegetables when you can. But there's no reason not to use canned fruit, because it gives off very little liquid and so doesn't soak the pastry crust. Be careful with frozen fruit: it contains a lot of water and this must be drained off before it can be arranged on the crust.

3. Taking your time

For your pastry to be in the best possible shape—malleable but not too elastic—it's best prepared a day ahead. Don't handle it too much when you work it, but give it the resting time it will need to hold well. Place it in the refrigerator for at least 3 hours after kneading. Ideally, it should be chilled overnight. Remove it from the refrigerator 15 minutes before rolling it out so that it's not too hard. Line the baking pan, and then return it for 30 minutes to the refrigerator. Otherwise, there'll be some nasty shrinkage during baking. It's a good idea to pre-bake it (also known as "baking blind"), the day before you need it, and finish the rest of the recipe the next day. This will give you a denser crust with more crunch.

4 Getting it right

Kneading

Knead the dough for the shortest possible time, using the food processor if you can. Then cover it in plastic wrap and chill. You must give the croissant pastry several "turns" once you have added the butter.

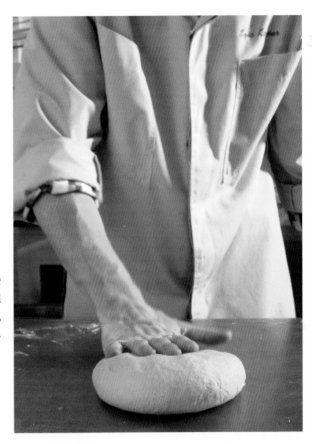

The dough must rise

Allow the dough to rise twice. This should be done for all types of dough that contain yeast: brioche, viennoise, fougasse, and croissant.

Sprinkle with flour

When preparing your working surface, sprinkle a little flour over it so that the dough doesn't stick. Be careful not to dust it too heavily, because that will make the dough heavier. The ideal working surface is marble: since it remains cool, it keeps the dough at the right temperature. You should also sprinkle your rolling pin lightly with flour.

Lining the baking pan

Your dough should always be rolled out into a disc, square, or rectangle that is slightly larger than the baking pan. Roll the dough around the rolling pin, and lay it gently in the pan. Lift the edge up with one hand while pressing lightly with the fingertips of the other hand to fit the dough into the bottom and against the sides of the pan.

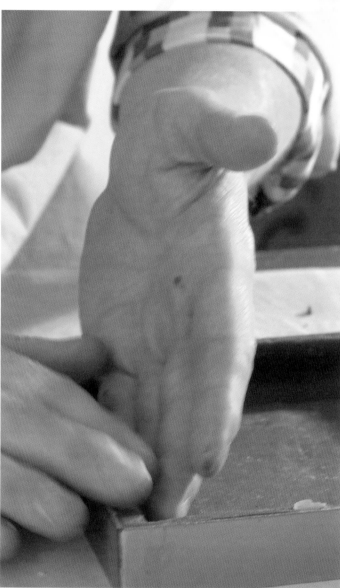

Trimming the dough

Don't roll your rolling pin over the pan to trim off the excess dough. Rather, cut it cleanly with a small, sharp knife that you hold at the edge of the pan. Turn the pan between the fingers of one hand, keeping the knife still.

ERIC KAYSER

My Quiches
and Savory Tarts

In winter, I love piping-hot quiches that melt in my mouth. In summer, I prefer to bite into tarts that are copiously garnished with luscious vegetables. The best accompaniment is always a crisp salad.

SMOKED TROUT
AND FENNEL TART

Ingredients

1 lb (400 g) savory pâte brisée (see recipe p. 20)
1 ¾ teaspoons (5 g) ground turmeric
5 large eggs
1 ¼ cups (300 ml) heavy cream
1 ¼ cups (300 ml) whole milk
juice of 1 lemon
juice of 2 oranges

Preparation time: 30 minutes   1 bunch of chives, snipped
Refrigeration time: overnight   1 ¾ lb fennel, stalks trimmed
Baking time: 1 hour   2 tablespoons olive oil
Baking pan: one 9 ½-inch (24-cm)   2 cucumbers
square or one 10-inch (26-cm)   ½ lb (250 g) smoked trout fillets
round pan.   Salt and freshly ground pepper to taste

 A day ahead (recommended)

Prepare the pâte brisée, adding turmeric to the flour. Cover in plastic wrap and refrigerate. In a mixing bowl, beat the eggs together with the heavy cream and the milk. Add the lemon juice and half the orange juice, and then the snipped chives. Mix well. (Reserve the rest of the orange juice for broiling the fennel.) Season with salt and pepper and leave in refrigerator.

 Prepare the filling

Preheat the oven to 400°F (210°C). Wash the fennel and slice it thinly. Broil the slices in the oven with the olive oil and the remaining orange juice for 15 minutes. Set aside to cool. Reduce the oven temperature to 350°F (180°C).

Cut the cucumbers lengthways in eight. Leave them in the refrigerator.
Line the baking pan with the pâte brisée and bake blind for 20 minutes (see p. 22).

Pour the cream and citrus juice mixture into the shell and bake for a further 25 minutes at 350°F (180°C). Set aside to cool.

Arrange the fennel slices on the tart, followed by the cucumber slices, and the trout fillets.

 Serve cool, with a green salad tossed
with a dressing flavored with orange juice.

FIELD MUSHROOM, FETA, AND CHERRY TOMATO QUICHE

Ingredients

1 lb (400 g) savory pâte brisée (see recipe p. 20)
1 bunch of mint, finely chopped
4 eggs
1 cup (250 ml) whole milk
1 cup (250 ml) heavy cream
½ lb (250 g) feta cheese
1 lb (500 g) field mushrooms or other wild mushrooms
Olive oil
1 lb (500 g) cherry tomatoes
Salt and freshly ground pepper to taste

Preparation time: 30 minutes
Refrigeration time: overnight
Baking time: 45 minutes
Baking pan: one 9 ½-inch (24-cm)
square or one 10-inch
(26-cm) round pan.

A day ahead (recommended)

Prepare the pâte brisée, adding ¼ cup (40 g) of the freshly chopped mint. Cover with plastic wrap and refrigerate.

In a mixing bowl, beat the eggs together with the milk and the heavy cream. Season with salt and pepper. Crumb the feta cheese into the mixture and add ⅓ cup (50 g) of freshly chopped mint. Cover the bowl with plastic wrap and refrigerate.

Prepare the filling

Preheat the oven to 350°F (180°C).

Wash and dry the mushrooms, and cut them into quarters. Sauté them lightly in a little olive oil until they turn a golden color, then add them to the egg and cream mixture.

Line the baking pan with the pastry and bake blind for 20 minutes (see p. 22).

Pour the mixture into the shell. Cut the cherry tomatoes in halves and arrange them on top of the quiche.

Bake for 25 minutes.

Serve hot, accompanied by a salad of Romaine lettuce with mint dressing.

LEEK, ANCHOVY, AND TAPENADE QUICHE

Ingredients

1 lb (400 g) savory pâte brisée (see recipe p. 20)
2 tablespoons (10 g) Herbes de Provence or mixed herbs,
  including thyme, rosemary, oregano, marjoram, etc.
4 large eggs
1 cup (250 ml) whole milk
1 cup (250 ml) heavy cream
100 g (3 oz) green olive tapenade
2 lb (1 kg) young leeks
3 oz (100 g) anchovies, canned in oil
Olive oil. Salt and freshly ground pepper to taste

Preparation time: 30 minutes
Refrigeration time: overnight
Baking time: 55 minutes
Baking pan: one 9½-inch (24-cm)
square or one 10-inch
(26-cm) round pan.

 A day ahead (recommended)

Prepare the pâte brisée, adding the herbs to the flour. Cover and refrigerate overnight.

In a mixing bowl, beat the eggs together with the milk and the heavy cream. Incorporate the green olive tapenade, and season with salt and pepper. Cover the bowl with wrap and refrigerate overnight.

 Prepare the filling

Preheat the oven to 350°F (180°C).

Wash and dry the leeks. Cut them in half, lengthways. Arrange them in an ovenproof dish and drizzle olive oil over them. Broil for about 10 minutes, until they turn a light golden color.

Line the baking pan with the pâte brisée and pre-bake for 20 minutes (see p. 22). Place the leeks in the shell and pour the prepared mixture over them. Bake for 25 minutes.

Drain the anchovies and arrange them on the quiche.

 Serve warm, accompanied by a rocket salad with basil dressing.

CHICKEN, EGGPLANT, AND COCONUT MILK TART

Ingredients

1 lb (400 g) savory pâte brisée (see recipe p. 20)
1 teaspoon (5 g) green curry paste
3 large eggs
¾ cup (200 ml) heavy cream
1 ⅔ cups (400 ml) coconut milk
1 ½ tablespoons (20 ml) soy sauce
1 lime (juice and zest)
1 lb (500 g) raw chicken breasts
3 eggplants
3 tablespoons olive oil
½ bunch of Thai basil
Salt and freshly ground pepper to taste

Preparation time: 35 minutes
Refrigeration time: overnight
Baking time: 55 minutes
Baking pan: one 9 ½-inch (24-cm) square or one 10-inch (26-cm) round pan.

 A day ahead (recommended)

Prepare the pâte brisée, incorporating the green curry paste. Cover in plastic wrap and refrigerate overnight. In a mixing bowl, beat the eggs together with the heavy cream and the coconut milk. Add the lime zest and juice and the soy sauce. Season with salt and pepper. Cover with plastic wrap and refrigerate overnight.

 Prepare the filling

Preheat the oven to 350°F (180°C). Dice the chicken breasts and add them to the egg mixture.

Cut the eggplants lengthways into about 12 slices each. Brush them with oil and broil in the oven for about 10 minutes, or until they turn a light golden color.

Line the baking pan with the pâte brisée and pre-bake it for 20 minutes (see p. 22). Arrange the eggplant slices in the pastry shell. Pour the chicken mixture over them and bake for 25 minutes.

Decorate with small leaves of the Thai basil.

 Serve warm, accompanied by a green papaya salad with Thai basil.

CURRIED CILANTRO ASPARAGUS QUICHE

Ingredients

Preparation time: 30 minutes
Refrigeration time: overnight
Baking time: 45 minutes
Baking pan: one 9½-inch (24-cm) square or one 10-inch (26-cm) round pan.

1 lb (400 g) savory pâte brisée (see recipe p. 20)
1 lb (400 g) green asparagus
3 large eggs
1 cup (250 ml) whole milk
1 ½ teaspoons (4 g) ground cilantro
1 teaspoon (4 g) green curry paste
1 ½ oz (40 g) grated Parmesan cheese
6 cherry tomatoes
Salt and freshly ground pepper to taste

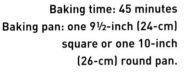

 A day ahead (recommended)

Prepare the pâte brisée. Cover it in plastic wrap and refrigerate. Blanch the asparagus in boiling water. Cut half the asparagus into small pieces and set aside the remaining half as whole stalks for the topping.

In a mixing bowl, beat the eggs together with the milk, the cilantro, and the curry paste.

Add the cut asparagus and the grated Parmesan. Season with salt and pepper. Cover the bowl with wrap and refrigerate overnight.

 Prepare the filling

Preheat the oven to 350°F (180°C).

Line the baking pan with the pâte brisée and bake blind for 20 minutes (see p. 22).

Pour the asparagus and Parmesan mixture into the crust. Arrange the remaining asparagus over the tart and decorate with the cherry tomato halves. Bake for 20 minutes.

 Serve warm or hot, accompanied by a mâche (lamb's lettuce) salad with cilantro dressing.

THREE-COLORED PEPPER
AND SMOKED HAM TART

Ingredients

1 lb (400 g) savory pâte brisée (see recipe p. 20)

2 tablespoons (10 g) Herbes de Provence or mixed herbs, including thyme, rosemary, oregano, marjoram, etc.

5 large eggs

1 cup plus 3 tablespoons (280 ml) heavy cream

1 cup plus 3 tablespoons (280 ml) whole milk

Preparation time: 20 minutes   2 cloves of garlic, finely chopped

Refrigeration time: overnight   ½ lb (200 g) smoked ham, finely chopped

Baking time: 1 hour 15 minutes   2 red bell peppers

Baking pan: one 9 ½-inch (24-cm)   2 yellow bell peppers

square or one 10-inch   2 green bell peppers

(26-cm) round pan.   Salt and freshly ground pepper to taste

A day ahead (recommended)

Prepare the pâte brisée, adding the herbs to the flour.
Cover in plastic wrap and refrigerate.

In a mixing bowl, beat the eggs with the cream and milk. Stir in the garlic and the smoked ham. Season with salt and pepper. Cover the bowl with plastic wrap and refrigerate overnight.

Prepare the filling

Preheat the oven to 400°F (210°C).

Broil the bell peppers, whole, in the oven for 30 minutes. Peel them, remove the seeds, and cut them into strips. Lower the oven temperature to 350°F (180°C).

Line the baking pan with the pâte brisée and bake blind for 20 minutes (see p. 22). Pour the mixture with the chopped ham into the crust and bake for 25 minutes at 350°F (180°C).

Arrange the bell pepper slices over the tart, alternating the red, yellow, and green.

Serve warm or cool with mixed salad greens scattered with toasted pine nuts.

CREAMED BEET
AND BROCCOLI QUICHE

Preparation time: 20 minutes
Refrigeration time: overnight
Baking time: 50 minutes
Baking pan: one 9 ½-inch (24-cm)
square or one 10-inch
(26-cm) round pan.

Ingredients

1 lb (400 g) savory pâte brisée (see recipe p. 20)
1 ½ tablespoons (10 g) allspice
3 large eggs
¾ cup (200 ml) heavy cream
¾ cup (200 ml) whole milk
1 lb (400 g) cooked, mashed beets
¾ lb (350 g) broccoli florets
Salt and freshly ground pepper to taste

 A day ahead (recommended)

Prepare the pâte brisée, adding the allspice to the flour. Cover in plastic wrap and refrigerate.

In a mixing bowl, beat the eggs with the cream and the milk. Add the puréed beetroot. Season with salt and pepper. Cover the bowl with wrap and refrigerate overnight.

 Prepare the filling

Preheat the oven to 350°F (180°C).

Blanch the broccoli: place the florets in boiling water for a few minutes. They should retain their crunch.

Line the baking pan with the pâte brisée and bake blind for 20 minutes (see p. 22). Arrange the broccoli florets in the shell and pour the beetroot mixture over. Bake for 25 minutes.

 Serve hot, accompanied by a radicchio salad with balsamic vinegar.

SWEET POTATO, GORGONZOLA, AND WALNUT QUICHE

Ingredients

1 lb (400 g) savory pâte brisée (see recipe p. 20)
1 ¾ teaspoons (5 g) ground turmeric, and a little extra for decoration
2 large eggs
⅔ cup heavy cream
⅔ cup whole milk
½ lb (200 g) gorgonzola
1 ¼ cups (150 g) chopped walnuts
2 lb (1 kg) sweet potatoes
Freshly ground pepper

Preparation time: 40 minutes
Refrigeration time: overnight
Baking time: 1 hour 20 minutes
Baking pan: one 9 ½-inch (24-cm)
square or one 10-inch (26-cm)
round pan.

A day ahead (recommended)

Prepare the pâte brisée, adding the turmeric to the flour.
Cover in plastic wrap and refrigerate.

In a mixing bowl, beat the eggs together with the cream and the milk. Cut up the gorgonzola, and incorporate it with the chopped walnuts into the mixture. Add freshly ground pepper to taste. Cover the bowl with wrap and refrigerate overnight.

Prepare the filling

Preheat the oven to 350°F (180°C).

Roast the sweet potatoes in the oven for 35 minutes. Scoop out the flesh and mash it.

Line the baking pan with the pâte brisée and bake blind for 20 minutes (see p. 22).

Spoon the mashed sweet potatoes into the shell, and then pour the gorgonzola-walnut mixture over this. Bake for 25 minutes.

Serve hot, sprinkled with turmeric, accompanied
by a lettuce salad with walnut oil.

PARMA HAM AND PEAR TART

Preparation time: 25 minutes
Refrigeration time: overnight
Baking time: 45 minutes
Baking pan: one 9 ½-inch (24-cm)
square or one 10-inch
(26-cm) round pan.

Ingredients

1 lb (400 g) savory pâte brisée (see recipe p. 20)
4 large eggs
1 cup (250 ml) heavy cream
1 cup (250 ml) whole milk
7 oz (200 g) chopped hazelnuts
2 ½ tablespoons (40 ml) balsamic vinegar
1 ¼ lb (600 g) pears
2 tablespoons (10 g) lemon-scented thyme
7 oz (200 g) thinly sliced Parma ham
Salt and freshly ground pepper to taste

A day ahead (recommended)

Prepare the pâte brisée. Cover in plastic wrap and refrigerate overnight.

In a mixing bowl, beat the eggs together with the cream and the milk. Add the chopped hazelnuts and the balsamic vinegar. Season with salt and pepper. Cover the bowl with plastic wrap and refrigerate overnight.

Prepare the filling

Preheat the oven to 350°F (180°C).

Cut the pears into 8 (or 12 if big), leaving them unpeeled. Sauté them with the lemon-scented thyme in a little olive oil until they turn a light golden color.

Line the baking pan with the pâte brisée and bake blind for 20 minutes (see p. 22).

Pour the hazelnut mixture into the shell and bake for 25 minutes.

Arrange the slices of Parma ham over the tart and top with the sautéed pear slices.

Serve cool, accompanied by a salad of oak-leaf lettuce with hazelnut oil.

GOAT-MILK CHEESE, ZUCCHINI, AND PINE NUT QUICHE

Preparation time: 15 minutes
Refrigeration time: overnight
Baking time: 55 minutes
Baking pan: one 9 ½-inch (24-cm)
square or one 10-inch
(26-cm) round pan.

Ingredients

1 lb (400 g) savory pâte brisée (see recipe p. 20)
¼ cup (40 g) finely chopped fresh mint
10 oz (300 g) zucchini
4 large eggs
¾ cup (200 ml) heavy cream
¾ cup (200 ml) whole milk
2 ½ oz (75 g) pine nuts, toasted
½ lb (200 g) mild, fresh chèvre (goat-milk) cheese, preferably log-shaped
Salt and freshly ground pepper to taste

A day ahead (recommended)

Prepare the pâte brisée, adding the chopped mint to the flour.
Cover in plastic wrap and refrigerate overnight.

Blanch the zucchini in boiling water for a few minutes.
Leaving the skin on, mash them coarsely.

In a mixing bowl, beat the eggs together with the cream and the milk. Add the puréed zucchini and 1 ½ oz (50 g) of the toasted pine nuts. Season with salt and pepper. Cover the bowl with plastic wrap and refrigerate overnight.

Prepare the filling

Preheat the oven to 350°F (180°C).

Line the baking pan with the pâte brisée and bake blind for 20 minutes (see p. 22).

Pour the zucchini mixture into the shell. Cut the goat-milk cheese into slices about ½ inch (1.5 cm) thick, and arrange them in rows on the filling. Bake for 25 minutes.

Scatter with remaining toasted pine nuts.

Serve hot or cool, accompanied by mixed salad greens with garlic dressing.

CHANTERELLE
AND DUCK BREAST TART

Ingredients

1 lb (400 g) savory pâte brisée (see recipe p. 20)
2 tablespoons (10 g) Herbes de Provence or mixed herbs, including thyme,
    rosemary, oregano, marjoram, etc.

Preparation time: 30 minutes
4 large eggs

Refrigeration time: overnight
1 cup (250 ml) whole milk

Baking time: 45 minutes
1 cup (250 ml) heavy cream

Baking pan: one 9 ½-inch (24-cm)
1 ½ lb (650 g) chanterelle or girolle mushrooms, or other wild mushrooms

square or one 10-inch (26-cm)
7 oz (200 g) duck breast, finely sliced, fat untrimmed

round pan.
Salt and freshly ground pepper to taste

 A day ahead (recommended)

Prepare the pâte brisée, adding the herbs to the flour.
Cover in plastic wrap and refrigerate.

In a mixing bowl, beat the eggs with the cream and the milk. Season with salt and pepper.
Cover the bowl with plastic wrap and refrigerate overnight.

 Prepare the filling

Preheat the oven to 350°F (180°C).

Line the baking pan with the pâte brisée and bake blind for 20 minutes (see p. 22).

Pour the cream mixture into the shell and bake for 25 minutes.
Wash the mushrooms and dry them using paper towel.

In a non-stick skillet, sauté the mushrooms with the fine slices of duck breast until they
all turn a golden color.

Arrange the mushrooms and the duck slices over the tart.

 Serve hot, accompanied by a mâche (lamb's lettuce) salad
with a blend of chopped parsley and garlic.

MARINATED SALMON AND MOZZARELLA TART

Ingredients

1 lb (400 g) fougasse pastry (see recipe p. 21)

2 tablespoons (10 g) Herbes de Provence or mixed herbs,
   including thyme, rosemary, oregano, marjoram, etc.

⅔ lb (300 g) salmon fillets, skinned

2 ½ oz (70 g) kosher salt

3 oz (80 g) granulated sugar

¾ teaspoon (2 g) mignonette pepper (equal parts of black and white pepper)

⅔ lb (300 g) mozzarella, preferably a cylindrical loaf

3 ½ oz (100 g) pesto

Salt and freshly ground pepper to taste

Preparation time: 30 minutes
Refrigeration time: overnight
Baking time: 20 minutes
Baking pan: one 9 ½-inch (24-cm)
square or one 10-inch
(26-cm) round pan.

A day ahead (recommended)

Incorporate the herbs into the dough. Form it into a ball, place in a bowl, and cover it with plastic wrap.

Rub the salmon with the kosher salt, the sugar, and the mignonette pepper. Cover with plastic wrap and refrigerate overnight.

Prepare the filling

Preheat the oven to 350°F (180°C).

Line the baking pan with the fougasse pastry and bake blind for 20 minutes (see p. 22). Set aside to cool.

Rinse the salmon and pat it dry. Cut it into slices about a ½-inch (1.5-cm) thick, and cut the mozzarella into slices of a similar thickness.

Spread the crust with pesto when it is cool. Alternate the salmon and mozzarella slices over the pesto in an attractive arrangement. Season with salt and pepper.

Serve cool with a vinaigrette comprising lemon juice, olive oil, and basil.

BLACK PUDDING AND APPLE QUICHE

Ingredients

1 lb (400 g) savory pâte brisée (see recipe p. 20)
1 ½ tablespoons (10 g) ground allspice
1 lb (500 g) peeled and diced apples, Granny Smith or other tart apples
¼ cup (50 g) unsalted butter
¼ cup (50 g) granulated sugar
2 large eggs
⅔ cup (150 ml) heavy cream
⅔ cup (150 ml) whole milk
1 lb (500 g) black pudding
Salt and freshly ground pepper to taste

Preparation time: 35 minutes
Refrigeration time: overnight
Baking time: 55 minutes
Baking pan: one 9 ½-inch
(24-cm) square.

 A day ahead (recommended)

Prepare the pâte brisée, incorporating the spices. Cover in plastic wrap and refrigerate overnight.

Sauté the apple cubes in the butter, together with the sugar, until they reach an apple sauce consistency. In a mixing bowl, beat the eggs with the cream and the milk. Season with salt and pepper. Add the apple sauce mixture. Cover the bowl with plastic wrap and refrigerate overnight.

 Prepare the filling

Preheat the oven to 350°F (180°C).

Line the baking pan with the pâte brisée and bake blind for 20 minutes (see p. 22). Cut the blood sausage lengthways in half and arrange it in the shell.

Pour the apple sauce mixture over the sausage and bake for 25 minutes.

 Serve hot with flat-leafed lettuce salad and shallot dressing.

ONION AND SAUSAGE TART
WITH BEAUJOLAIS WINE

Ingredients

1 lb (400 g) savory pâte brisée (see recipe p. 20)
2 teaspoons (5 g) ground cinnamon
4 large eggs
¾ cup (200 ml) heavy cream
¾ cup (200 ml) whole milk
1 cup (250 ml) Beaujolais wine or other fruity red wine
3 oz (100 g) rosette de Lyon or other dry pork sausage, diced
4 red onions
6 Belgian endives
Salt and freshly ground pepper to taste

Preparation time: 25 minutes
Refrigeration time: overnight
Baking time: 45 minutes
Baking pan: one 9 ½-inch (24-cm)
square or one 10-inch
(26-cm) round pan.

 A day ahead (recommended)

Prepare the pâte brisée, adding the cinnamon. Cover in plastic wrap and refrigerate overnight.

In a mixing bowl, beat the eggs together with the cream, the milk, and the wine. Add the diced dry sausage. Season with salt and pepper. Cover the bowl with plastic wrap and refrigerate overnight.

 Prepare the filling

Preheat the oven to 350°F (180°C).

Line the baking pan with the pâte brisée and bake blind for 20 minutes (see p. 22).

Cut the onions into eight, and the Belgian endives into quarters. Arrange them in the shell. Pour the wine and sausage mixture over and bake for 25 minutes.

 Serve hot, accompanied by a salad of frisée
or other bitter leaves seasoned with cider vinegar.

ZUCCHINI AND BRAISED LETTUCE TART

Ingredients

Preparation time: 30 minutes
Refrigeration time: overnight
Baking time: 40 minutes
Baking pan: one 9 inch (24-cm)
square or one 10 inch
(26-cm) round pan.

1 lb (400 g) savory pâte brisée (see recipe p. 20)
1 lettuce, butterhead or romaine
Olive oil
1 clove garlic
2 zucchini
4 oz (120 g) tapenade
Salt and freshly ground pepper to taste

 A day ahead (recommended)

Prepare the pâte brisée, cover in plastic wrap, and chill overnight.

 Prepare the filling

Preheat oven to 350°F (180°C).

Line the baking pan with the pâte brisée and pre-bake for 20 minutes (see p. 22).

Wash and spin-dry the lettuce leaves. Braise them in a pot with a little olive oil, salt, and pepper. Crush the garlic clove into the pot and mix through.

Cook on a low heat for 20 minutes, until all the water has evaporated.

Wash the zucchini and slice thinly, lengthways. Place the slices in an ovenproof dish and drizzle olive oil over them. Season with salt and pepper, and broil in the oven for 10 minutes. Turn slices over to broil the other side. Set aside to cool.

Spread the tapenade over the crust. Arrange a layer of cooled zucchini slices, and cover with cooled braised lettuce. Alternate layers of zucchini and lettuce, finishing with zucchini.

 Serve cool, accompanied by a tomato salad
with grilled pine nuts, and basil dressing.

OYSTER MUSHROOM AND BACON BIT QUICHE

Ingredients

1 lb (400 g) fougasse dough (see recipe p. 21)
3 large eggs
¾ cup (200 ml) heavy cream
¾ cup (200 ml) whole milk
3 cloves of garlic, finely chopped
3 ½ oz (100 g) chervil, finely chopped
¾ lb (350 g) oyster mushrooms (pleurotes)
½ lb (200 g) bacon bits
Salt and freshly ground pepper to taste

Preparation time: 20 minutes
Refrigeration time: overnight
Baking time: 45 minutes
Baking pan: one 9 ½-inch (24-cm)
square or one 10-inch
(26-cm) round pan.

A day ahead (recommended)

Prepare the fougasse dough, cover in plastic wrap, and chill overnight.
In a mixing bowl, beat the eggs together with the cream, the milk, the chopped garlic, and the chopped chervil. Season with salt and pepper. Cover the bowl with plastic wrap and place in refrigerator overnight.

Prepare the filling

Preheat oven to 350°F (180°C).

Line the baking pan with the fougasse dough and pre-bake for 20 minutes (see p. 22).

Wash the mushrooms and dry them. Arrange them in the shell.
In a skillet, sauté the bacon bits until they turn golden brown. Add them to the cream and herb mixture.

Pour the mixture over the mushrooms and bake for 25 minutes.

Serve hot, accompanied by a dandelion salad dressed with mixed fresh herbs.

TOMATO TRIO

Ingredients

1 lb (400 g) fougasse dough (see recipe p. 21)

2 tablespoons (10 g) Herbes de Provence or mixed herbs, including thyme, rosemary, oregano, marjoram, etc.

4 large eggs

1 cup (250 ml) heavy cream

1 cup (250 ml) whole milk

¼ lb (130 g) sun dried tomato paste

4 tomatoes, peeled, seeded, and diced

3 garlic cloves, finely chopped

10 oz (300 g) tomatoes, quartered and slow-roasted with olive oil

Salt and freshly ground pepper to taste

Preparation time: 20 minutes
Baking time: 45 minutes
Refrigeration time: overnight
Baking pan: one 9 ½-inch (24-cm) square or one 10-inch (26-cm) round pan.

 A day ahead (recommended)

Incorporate the herbs into the dough. Form it into a ball, place it in a bowl, and cover with plastic wrap. Refrigerate overnight.

In a mixing bowl, beat the eggs together with the cream and the milk. Add the tomato paste, the diced tomatoes, and the chopped garlic. Season with salt and pepper. Cover the bowl with plastic wrap and place in refrigerator overnight.

 Prepare the filling

Preheat oven to 350°F (180°C).

Line the baking pan with the fougasse dough and pre-bake for 20 minutes (see p. 22).

Arrange the roasted tomatoes in the shell. Pour the tomato and cream mixture into the shell and bake for 25 minutes.

Serve warm or hot, accompanied by spinach shoots with Parmesan shavings.

ARTICHOKE, TAPENADE, AND PARMESAN QUICHE

Ingredients

1 lb (400 g) savory pâte brisée (see recipe p. 20)
1 tablespoon (5 g) fennel seeds
3 large eggs
¾ cup (200 ml) heavy cream
¾ cup (200 ml) whole milk
3 ½ oz (100 g) black olive tapenade
10 fresh artichoke hearts
½ lemon
3 ½ oz (100 g) Parmesan shavings
Salt and freshly ground pepper to taste

Preparation time: 30 minutes
Refrigeration time: overnight
Baking time: 55 minutes
Baking pan: one 9 ½-inch (24-cm)
square or one 10-inch
(26-cm) round pan.

A day ahead (recommended)

Prepare the pâte brisée, adding the fennel seeds. Cover with plastic wrap and chill overnight. In a mixing bowl, beat the eggs together with the cream and the milk. Stir in the tapenade, and season with salt and pepper. Cover the bowl with plastic wrap and place in refrigerator overnight.

Prepare the filling

Preheat the oven to 350°F (180°C).

Add salt and the lemon half to the boiling water and cook the artichoke hearts for 15 minutes, or until they start to soften (test with a fork).

Line the baking pan with the pâte brisée and bake blind for 20 minutes (see p. 22).
Cut the artichoke hearts in two and arrange them in the shell.
Pour the cream mixture over the artichoke hearts and bake for 25 minutes.
Scatter Parmesan shavings over the quiche.

Serve warm or hot with a salad of mixed greens and black olives.

CHICKEN LIVER
AND CARROT TART

Ingredients

1 lb (400 g) savory pâte brisée (see recipe p. 20)
5 tablespoons (50 g) black sesame seeds, and a little more for decoration
3 large eggs
¾ cup (200 ml) heavy cream
¾ cup (200 ml) whole milk
1 tablespoon (10g) pink peppercorns, crushed
1 ¾ lb (800 g) chicken livers
2 tablespoons (30 g) unsalted butter
5 carrots, peeled and very thinly sliced
Salt to taste

Preparation time: 25 minutes
Refrigeration time: overnight
Baking time: 55 minutes
Baking pan: one 9 ½-inch (24-cm)
square or one 10-inch
(26-cm) round pan.

 A day ahead (recommended)

Prepare the pâte brisée, adding 1 tablespoon (10 g) of the sesame seeds.
Cover with plastic wrap and chill overnight.

In a mixing bowl, beat the eggs together with the cream and the milk. Add the remaining 4 tablespoons (40 g) of sesame seeds and the crushed pink peppercorns, and season with salt. Cover the bowl with plastic wrap and place in refrigerator overnight.

 Prepare the filling

Preheat oven to 350°F (180°C).

Lightly brown the chicken livers in the butter. Line the baking pan with the pâte brisée and bake blind for 20 minutes (see p. 22).

Arrange the cooked chicken livers and carrot slices in the shell.

Pour the sesame seed and peppercorn mixture over and bake for 25 minutes.

 Serve hot, scattered with sesame seeds, accompanied by a salad of Belgian endives with sesame oil.

SCALLOP
AND ZUCCHINI TART

Ingredients

Preparation time: 15 minutes
Refrigeration time: overnight
Baking time: 25 minutes
Baking pan: one 9 ½-inch (24-cm)
square or one 10-inch
(26-cm) round pan.

1 lb (400 g) fougasse dough (see recipe p. 21)
7 oz (200 g) zucchini, thinly sliced lengthways
1 clove garlic
7 oz (200 g) canned coarsely chopped tomatoes
10 oz (300 g) scallops
3 tablespoons oil
1 bunch chives
Salt and freshly ground pepper to taste

A day ahead (recommended)

Prepare the fougasse dough. Cover in plastic wrap and refrigerate.
Broil or grill the zucchini slices.

Prepare the filling

Preheat the oven to 350°F (180°C). Line the baking pan with the fougasse dough and pre-bake for 20 minutes (see p. 22).

Crush the garlic clove into the chopped tomatoes. Season the tomatoes with salt and pepper. Spoon the mixture into the tart shell. Cover with the zucchini slices.

Finely slice the scallops. Sauté them lightly in a nonstick skillet with the oil for no more than 1 minute on each side.

Remove the scallops from the skillet and arrange them immediately on the tart. Season with salt and pepper. Scatter with snipped chives.

Serve warm, accompanied by a salad of fresh chopped herbs.

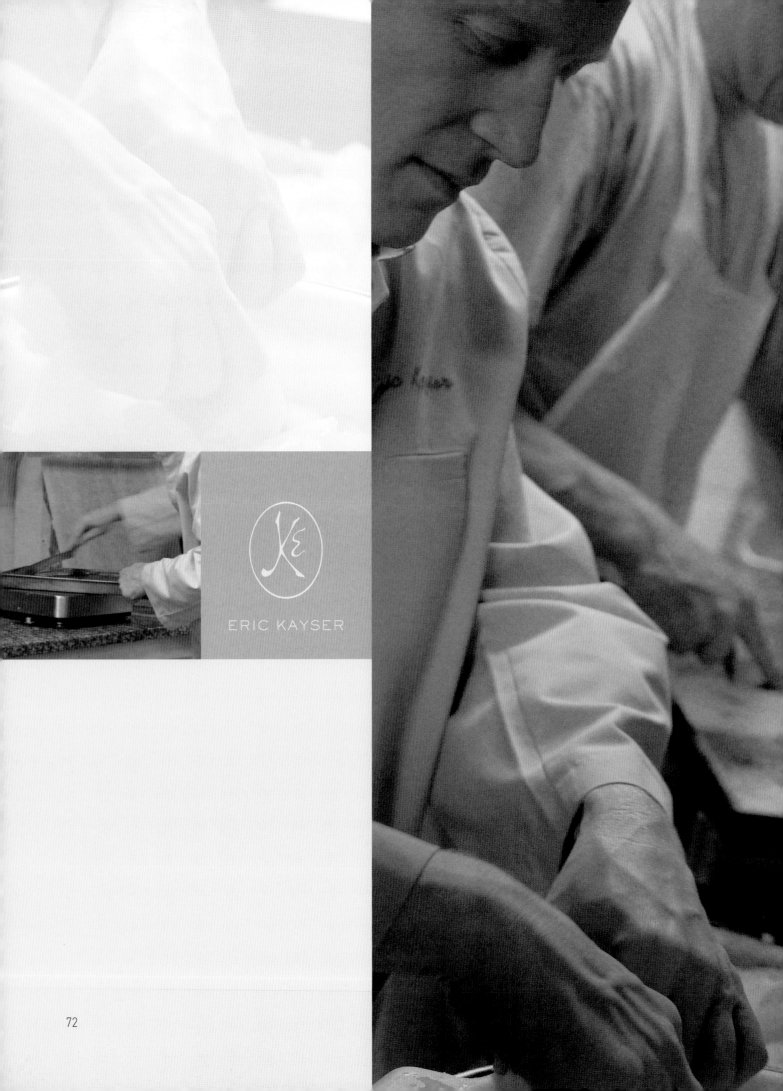

ERIC KAYSER

My Fruit Tarts

I often start by eating the fruit, keeping the crust —the best part—for last...unless it's smothered in a delectable cream, in which case I forget my manners and devour it all together with gusto.

PEAR AND GRAPEFRUIT TART

Ingredients

10 oz (300 g) almond shortbread pastry (see recipe p. 12)
4 to 5 pink grapefruit to yield 10 oz (300 g) segments
1 lb (500 g) canned pear halves
½ cup (125 g) unsalted butter, softened
⅔ cup (125 g) granulated sugar
1 ½ cups (125 g) ground almonds
2 tablespoons (10 g) flour
3 eggs
1 oz (30 g) pistachio paste
2 tablespoons apricot jam

Preparation time: 40 minutes
Baking time: 35 minutes
Baking pan: one rectangular
12 x 8-inch (20 x 30-cm) pan
or one round 10-inch (26-cm) pan.

Preheat the oven to 325°F (160°C).

Line the baking pan with the almond shortbread pastry.
Peel the grapefruit, removing all white pith. Separate into segments and remove
the membranes. Drain the canned pears. Cut each one lengthways into three slices.

In a mixing bowl, cream the butter. Combine the sugar, the ground almonds, and the flour
with the butter. Mix until the consistency is smooth. Add eggs one by one, beating all the
time, and then incorporate the pistachio paste.

Pour the mixture into the pastry shell. Arrange the fruit over this, alternating pear slices
and grapefruit segments.

Bake for 35 minutes.

Leave to cool. Soften the apricot jam in a saucepan over low heat.
Glaze the tart evenly.

CHERRY CLAFOUTIS TART

Ingredients

10 oz (300 g) shortbread pastry (see recipe p. 11)
1 lb (400 g) fresh morello cherries (alternatively, frozen or canned but unpitted)
2 whole eggs
4 egg yolks
1 cup (200 g) granulated sugar
¾ cup (60 g) ground almonds
⅔ cup (60 g) flour
¾ cup (200 ml) whole milk
2 ⅔ cups (400 g) heavy cream (30–40 percent butterfat, or crème fraîche)
1 ½ teaspoons (8 g) pure vanilla extract

Preparation time: 20 minutes
Baking time: 40 minutes
Baking pan: one rectangular
12 x 8-inch (20 x 30-cm) pan or one
round 10-inch (26-cm) pan.

Preheat the oven to 300°F (150°C).

Line the baking pan with the shortbread pastry.

Wash the cherries, remove the stalks, and dry them, without removing the pits.
In a mixing bowl, beat the whole eggs and the yolks together with the sugar.

Add the ground almonds and the flour, beating constantly. Then add the milk, continuing to beat at a high speed to avoid lumps forming. Incorporate the cream and the vanilla extract.

Arrange the cherries on the shell. Pour the mixture over the cherries and bake for 40 minutes.

Serve warm or cool.

BLUEBERRY TART

Ingredients

10 oz (300 g) almond shortbread pastry (see recipe p. 12)
1 lb (500 g) blueberries
½ cup (125 g) unsalted butter, softened
⅔ cup (125 g) granulated sugar
1 ½ cups (125 g) ground almonds
2 tablespoons (10 g) flour
3 eggs
2 teaspoons (10 g) gold rum
2 tablespoons blueberry jam
Confectioners' sugar

Preparation time: 20 minutes
Baking time: 30 minutes
Baking pan: one rectangular
12 x 8-inch (20 x 30-cm) pan
or one round 10-inch (26-cm) pan.

Preheat the oven to 325°F (160°C).

Line the baking pan with the almond shortbread pastry. Carefully wash the blueberries and dry them using paper towel. In a mixing bowl, cream the butter.

Add the sugar, the ground almonds, the flour, and mix in the eggs one by one. Mix until the batter is smooth. Stir in the rum.

Pour the batter over and bake for 30 minutes. Allow to cool.

In a saucepan, soften the jam. Remove from heat and gently roll the blueberries in the liquefied jam. Arrange the blueberries on the top of the tart. Dust the edges with confectioners' sugar.

NORMANDY APPLE TART

Ingredients

10 oz (300 g) shortbread pastry (see recipe p. 11)
1 ¼ lb (600 g) apples (preferably firm and tart, such as Granny Smith)
2 tablespoons (30 g) unsalted butter
1 ¼ cups (250 g) granulated sugar
1 teaspoon (3 g) ground cinnamon
2 whole eggs
4 egg yolks
¾ cup (60 g) ground almonds
⅔ cup (60 g) flour
½ pint (200 ml) whole milk
1 ⅔ cups (400 g) heavy cream (30–40 percent butterfat) or crème fraîche
1 ½ teaspoons (8 g) pure vanilla extract
Confectioners' sugar

Preparation time: 30 minutes
Baking time: 40 minutes
Baking pan: one rectangular
12 x 8-inch (20 x 30-cm) pan or one
round 10-inch (26-cm) pan.

Preheat the oven to 325°F (160°C).

Line the baking pan with the shortbread pastry. Peel the apples and slice them into pieces about ½ inch (1 cm) thick.

Melt the butter in a nonstick skillet. Place apples in the skillet, and sprinkle with ¼ cup (50 g) sugar and the cinnamon. Sauté the apple slices until they begin to soften and turn golden.

In a mixing bowl, beat the whole eggs and the yolks together with 1 cup (200 g) granulated sugar. Add the ground almonds and the flour, beating constantly. Then add the milk, beating vigorously so that no lumps form. Fold in the cream and the vanilla extract.

Arrange the apple slices in the shell and pour the mixture over them.
Bake for 40 minutes.

 Allow to cool. To serve, sprinkle with confectioners' sugar.

DAMSON
PLUM TART

Preparation time: 20 minutes
Baking time: 50 minutes
Baking pan: one rectangular
12 x 8-inch (20 x 30-cm) pan
or one round 10-inch (26-cm) pan.

Ingredients

250 g (½ lb) almond shortbread pastry (see recipe p. 12)
2 lb (1 kg) damson plums
3 eggs
1 ¼ cups (250 g) granulated sugar
1 cup (80 g) ground almonds
1 tablespoon (8 g) ground cinnamon, and a little more for decoration
½ cup (100 ml) whipping cream
3 tablespoons (40 g) unsalted butter, melted
Confectioners' sugar

Preheat the oven to 325°F (160°C).

Line the pan with the almond shortbread pastry. Pre-bake for 30 minutes (see p. 22).
Remove from oven and set aside to cool.

Wash the plums and dry them with paper towel. Cut them all in two and remove the stones.

In a mixing bowl, beat the eggs together with the sugar. Add the ground almonds, the
cinnamon, and the whipping cream. Mix through. Add the melted butter and stir until blended.

Pour half the batter into the shell and arrange the plum halves on it.
Pour the rest of the batter over the plums and bake for 20 minutes.

 Serve cool, decorated with a mixture of icing sugar and cinnamon.

APRICOT
PISTACHIO TART

Preparation time: 30 minutes
Baking time: 25 minutes
Baking pan: one rectangular
12 x 8-inch (20 x 30-cm) pan
or one round 10-inch (26-cm) pan.

Ingredients

10 oz (300 g) almond shortbread pastry (see recipe p. 12)
1 ½ lb (700 g) canned apricots
½ cup (125 g) unsalted butter, softened
⅔ cup (125 g) granulated sugar
1 ½ cups (125 g) ground almonds
2 tablespoons (10 g) flour
3 eggs
1 oz (30 g) pistachio paste
1 oz (30 g) chopped, unsalted pistachios

Preheat the oven to 325°F (160°C).

Line a baking pan with the almond shortbread pastry. Drain the canned apricots.

In a mixing bowl, cream the softened butter. Add the sugar, the ground almonds, and the flour. Mix until all ingredients are thoroughly blended.

Add the eggs, one by one, beating all the time. Add the pistachio paste, mixing well.

Pour half the mixture into the pastry shell. Arrange the apricots, cut side up and overlapping, and cover with the rest of the mixture. Bake for 25 minutes.

 Scatter chopped pistachios over the top and serve cool.

MIRABELLE
ALMOND TART

Preparation time: 25 minutes
Baking time: 35 minutes
Baking pan: one rectangular
12 x 8-inch (20 x 30-cm) pan
or one round 10-inch (26-cm) pan.

½ lb (250 g) almond shortbread pastry
1 ½ lb (700 g) Mirabelle plums
3 eggs
1 ¼ cups (250 g) granulated sugar
1 cup (80 g) ground almonds
1 tablespoon (8 g) ground cinnamon
½ cup (100 ml) cup whipping cream
3 tablespoons (40 g) unsalted butter, melted
1 oz (30 g) flaked almonds

Preheat the oven to 325°F (160°C). Line the baking pan with the almond shortbread pastry. Wash the Mirabelles and dry them on a paper towel. Remove pits.

In a mixing bowl, beat the eggs and the sugar together. Add the ground almonds, cinnamon, and whipping cream. Mix together, and then pour in melted butter. Mix again.

Arrange the Mirabelles on the shell cut side down and pour the mixture over them.

Scatter with flaked almonds. Bake for 35 minutes.

 Serve cool.

STRAWBERRIES ON PISTACHIO DACQUOISE

Ingredients

Butter for the mold
½ lb (240 g) pistachio dacquoise pastry (see recipe p. 16)
1 oz (30 g) unsalted chopped pistachios
1 ½ lb (700 g) strawberries
1 cup (250 ml) whole milk
3 egg yolks
¼ cup (50 g) granulated sugar
¼ cup (25g) flour plus a little for the baking pan
1 ½ tablespoons (15 g) cornstarch
½ cup (100 ml) whipping cream

Preparation time: 35 minutes
Baking time: 35 minutes
Baking pan: one rectangular
12 x 8-inch (20 x 30-cm) pan
or one round 10-inch (26-cm) pan.

Preheat the oven to 350°F (170°C)

Wash, hull, and dry the strawberries. Cut them in half lengthways.

In a saucepan, bring the milk to the boil. In a mixing bowl, beat the egg yolks together with the sugar, the flour, and the cornstarch.

Pour a little boiling milk into this mixture, beat, and return it all into the saucepan.

Bring the mixture back to the boil, stirring constantly with a wooden spoon. Remove from heat and set aside to cool.

Butter the mold and dust it with flour. Line the pan with the dacquoise pastry.

Sprinkle the pastry with chopped pistachios, setting aside some for decoration. Bake for 25 minutes. Set aside to cool.

Whip the cream, and fold it into the cooled milk mixture. Spoon it over the dacquoise.

Arrange the strawberries, and garnish with the remaining chopped pistachios.

RHUBARB
AND ORANGE TART

Ingredients

10 oz (300 g) almond shortbread pastry (see recipe p. 12)
2 lb (1 kg) fresh rhubarb stalks
2 oranges, preferably organic
2 pints (1 liter) water
½ cup (125 g) unsalted butter, softened
1 lb (450 g) granulated sugar
1 ¾ cups (150 g) ground almonds
¼ cup (20 g) flour
3 eggs
4 teaspoons (20 ml) Grand Marnier
Confectioners' sugar for decoration

Preparation time: 45 minutes
Baking time: 30 minutes
Baking pan: one rectangular
12 x 8-inch (20 x 30-cm) pan
or one round 10-inch (26-cm) pan.

Preheat the oven to 325°F (160°C).

Line the baking pan with the almond shortbread pastry. Wash and trim the rhubarb.
Cut into 1-inch (2-cm) slices. Finely grate the zest of the oranges.

Bring 2 pints of water to the boil in a saucepan, and add the rhubarb together with 1 ½ cups
(300 g) granulated sugar. Bring the mixture to the boil again. Strain the rhubarb in a colander
for approximately 30 minutes.

In a mixing bowl, cream the butter. Add ¾ cup (150 g) granulated sugar, the ground
almonds and the flour, and then the eggs, one by one. Mix until all ingredients are thoroughly
incorporated. Stir in the grated orange zest and the Grand Marnier.

Spoon the rhubarb into the pastry shell. Pour the mixture over the rhubarb and bake for
30 minutes.

 Serve cool, dusted with confectioners' sugar.

MATCHA GREEN TEA
AND RED CURRANT TART

Preparation time: 25 minutes
Baking time: 30 minutes
Baking pan: one rectangular
12 x 8-inch (20 x 30-cm) pan
or one round 10-inch (26-cm) pan.

Ingredients

1 ⅓ cup (300 g) unsalted butter
10 egg whites
2 ¼ cups (300 g) confectioners' sugar
1 ½ cups (130 g) ground almonds
1 ½ cups (130 g) flour
2 teaspoons green matcha tea, and a little more for decoration
13 oz (375 g) red currants
2 tablespoons red currant jelly

Preheat the oven to 350°F (170°C).

In a saucepan, melt the butter until it starts to turn a nut-brown color. Remove immediately from heat.

In a mixing bowl, whip the egg whites with the confectioners' sugar.

Add the ground almonds, the flour, and the green tea.

Mix together, and add the melted butter (it must still be hot), stirring constantly.

Pour the mixture into the pan till about three-quarters full. Bake for 30 minutes.

Remove from oven and set aside to cool.

Soften the red currant jelly in a small saucepan over low heat. Remove the red currants from their stalks and mix them with the liquefied jelly. Spoon them over the pastry and sprinkle with matcha green tea.

PINEAPPLE COCONUT TART

Ingredients

10 oz (300 g) almond shortbread pastry (see recipe p. 12)
1 2/3 cups (400 ml) coconut milk
4 egg yolks
1/4 cup (50 g) granulated sugar
1/3 cup cornstarch (60 g) cornstarch
1 large pineapple
2/3 cup (150 ml) heavy cream (30% butterfat) or crème fraîche
1/3 cup (30 g) coconut flakes

Preparation time: 45 minutes
Baking time: 30 minutes
One 10-inch (26-cm) baking pan.

Preheat the oven to 325°F (160°C).

Line the baking pan with the almond shortbread pastry.

Bake blind for 30 minutes (see p. 22).

Remove from oven and allow to cool.

In a saucepan, bring the coconut milk to the boil. In a mixing bowl, beat the yolks together with the sugar and the cornstarch. Still beating, pour the coconut milk into the mixture.

Pour back into the saucepan and bring just up to the boil again, stirring constantly.

Remove from heat and set aside to cool.

Peel the pineapple and cut it into quarters, lengthways. Remove the hard center core and cut the fruit into small cubes.

Whip the cream and fold it into the coconut milk mixture, which should now be cool.

Spoon into the tart shell. Cover the mixture with the pineapple cubes and decorate with coconut flakes.

TANGERINE
AND ALMOND CREAM TART

Preparation time: 30 minutes
Baking time: 45 minutes
Baking pan: one 9-inch (24-cm)
square or one 10-inch
(26-cm) round pan.

Ingredients

7 oz (200 g) almond shortbread pastry (see recipe p. 12)
7 tangerines
1 ¼ cups (250 g) granulated sugar
3 tablespoons (40 g) unsalted butter, melted
3 eggs
1 cup (80 g) ground almonds
½ cup (100 ml) whipping cream
Confectioners' sugar for decoration

Preheat the oven to 325°F (160°C).

Line the baking pan with the almond shortbread pastry and bake blind for 20 minutes (see p. 22). Set aside to cool.

Peel 6 of the tangerines and separate into segments.

Arrange them over the pastry shell once it has cooled. In a mixing bowl, beat together 1 cup (200 g) granulated sugar with the melted butter.

Then add the eggs, one by one, continuing to whip. Carefully incorporate the ground almonds and the whipping cream.

Pour this mixture over the tangerine segments. Bake for 25 minutes.

Allow the tart to cool. Peel the remaining tangerine. In a skillet, heat the segments lightly for a few seconds with the remaining ¼ cup (50 g) sugar and decorate the tart with them.

 Dust the tart with confectioners' sugar.

MANGO UPSIDE-DOWN CAKE

Preparation time: 20 minutes
Baking time: 1 hour
Resting time: 10 minutes
One 9 inch-round cake pan.

Ingredients

¾ cup (150 g) granulated sugar
5 tablespoons (75 g) butter, cut into small cubes
1 teaspoon ground ginger
2 firm mangoes
7 oz (200 g) croissant pastry (see recipe p. 17)
⅔ cup (150 cl) whipping cream, ginger, and lime zest for garnish

Preheat the oven to 325°F (160°C).

Melt the granulated sugar in the pan until it reaches a light caramel color. Gradually incorporate the butter, together with the ginger. Set aside to cool.

Peel the mangoes. Cut them into slices working round the pit, and arrange them in a pinwheel in the cake pan. Bake for 30 minutes.

Remove the juice that has run off from the fruit during the baking. Cover the mango slices with the croissant pastry. Prick it with a fork and return to oven for another 30 minutes.

Allow the tart to cool off slightly for 10 minutes before turning it over onto a serving platter.

 Serve immediately with whipped cream flavored with ground ginger and lime zest.

MIXED BERRY TART

Preparation time: 30 minutes
Refrigeration: 1 hour
Baking time: 35 minutes
Baking pan: one rectangular
12 x 8-inch (20 x 30-cm) pan or one
round 10-inch (26-cm) pan.

Ingredients

10 oz (300 g) shortbread crust (see recipe p. 11)
3 ¼ sheets (8 g) leaf gelatin
2 ¾ cups (400 g) heavy cream (30 percent butterfat) or crème fraîche
⅔ cup (80 g) confectioners' sugar
4 teaspoons (20 g) kirsch
14 oz or approx. 3 ⅓ cups total (400 g) farmer's cheese,
    mixed with a little cream (or fromage blanc)
1 ¾ lb (800 g) assorted raspberries, strawberries,
    mulberries, red currants, and blueberries.

Preheat the oven to 350°F (180°C).

Line the pan with the shortbread crust. Bake blind for 35 minutes (see p. 22).
Remove from oven and set aside to cool.

Soak the leaves of gelatin in a bowl of cold water.

Whip the cream together with the confectioners' sugar until it forms soft peaks.
Slightly warm the kirsch in a small saucepan.

Remove the gelatin from the water and squeeze the leaves to remove all excess water.

Remove the kirsch from the heat and add the gelatin to it, stirring well until it is
thoroughly dissolved.

Incorporate the gelatin-kirsch liquid into the cream cheese, then gently fold in the
whipped cream using a wooden spoon or spatula.

Pour this mixture into the pastry crust, now cool, and refrigerate for 1 hour.

To serve, gently wash and dry the berries. Arrange them attractively over the tart.

QUINCE TART
WITH MEAD

Ingredients

½ lb (250 g) shortbread crust (see recipe p. 11)
4 quinces
2 ¼ cups (425 g) granulated sugar
3 eggs
1 ½ cups (125 g) ground almonds
¼ cup (20 g) cake flour
1 ½ tablespoons (20 ml) gold rum
½ cup (125 g) unsalted butter, melted
2 tablespoons quince jelly
½ cup (100 ml) mead (honey wine)
2 pints (1 liter) water
Flaked almonds

Preparation time: 25 minutes
Refrigeration time: 15 minutes
Baking time: 1 hour
Baking pan: one 9-inch (24-cm)
square or one round 10-inch
(26-cm) round pan.

Preheat the oven to 325°F (160°C).

Line the baking pan with the shortbread pastry and refrigerate.

Peel the quinces. Cut them in half and remove the cores. Slice each half into thick slices. Boil the pieces for 40 minutes in 2 pints (1 liter) of water with 1 ½ cup (300 g) sugar. Drain and set aside.

In a mixing bowl, beat the eggs with the remaining ⅔ cup (125 g) sugar. Incorporate the ground almonds, the flour, and the rum. Mix thoroughly and then pour in the melted butter. Mix through again. Spoon this mixture into the pastry shell.

Arrange the quince slices attractively on top of the mixture and bake for 20 minutes. Soften the quince jelly over a low heat, so that it is liquefied when you remove the tart from the oven. Spread the jelly over the tart immediately, and then pour the mead over liberally.

 Serve warm, scattered with flaked almonds.

PEAR
AND FIG TART

Ingredients

10 oz (300 g) almond shortbread pastry (see recipe p. 12)
1 lb (500 g) canned pear halves
1 lb (500 g) fresh figs
½ cup (125 g) unsalted butter, softened
⅔ cup (125 g) granulated sugar
1 ½ cups (125 g) ground almonds
2 tablespoons (10 g) cake flour
3 eggs
1 oz (30 g) pistachio paste
2 tablespoons apricot jam

Preparation time: 30 minutes
Baking time: 25 minutes
Baking pan: one rectangular
12 x 8-inch (20 x 30-cm) pan
or one round 10-inch (26-cm) pan.

Preheat the oven to 325°F (160°C).

Line the pan with the almond shortbread pastry.

Drain the canned pears. Cut them lengthways into three. Wash the figs and dry them using paper towel. Cut them into quarters.

In a mixing bowl, cream the butter, and add the sugar, ground almonds, and flour. Beat until all the ingredients are thoroughly mixed.

Add the eggs, one by one, beating constantly, then incorporate the pistachio paste.

Pour the mixture into the pastry shell. Arrange the fruit, alternating pear slices and fig quarters, setting aside a few figs for decoration. Bake for 25 minutes. Allow to cool. Soften the apricot jam over a low heat, and brush over the tart.

 Decorate with remaining fig quarters.

COCONUT, PAPAYA, AND PINEAPPLE TART

Preparation time: 35 minutes
Baking time: 30 minutes
Baking pan: one 9-inch (24-cm)
square pan
or one 10-inch (26-cm) round pan.

Ingredients
½ lb (250 g) almond shortbread pastry (see recipe p. 12)
1 cup (250 ml) coconut milk
3 egg yolks
¼ cup (50 g) granulated sugar
3 tablespoons (30 g) cornstarch
1 large pineapple
3 papayas
½ cup (100 g) heavy cream (30 percent butterfat) or crème fraîche
1 oz (30 g) fresh, shredded coconut, for decoration

Preheat the oven to 325°F (160°C).

Line the pan with the almond shortbread pastry.

Bake blind for 30 minutes (see p. 22). Remove from oven and set aside to cool.

In a saucepan, bring the coconut milk to the boil. In a mixing bowl, beat the egg yolks together with the sugar and the cornstarch. Pour the coconut milk into this mixture, beating thoroughly, and then pour combined ingredients back into saucepan. Bring up to a simmer again, take off the heat, and cool quickly by placing the pan in iced water.

Peel the pineapple and cut it into four lengthways. Remove the hard central core. Cut each quarter lengthways again into three slices. Peel the papayas, cut them into four, and remove the seeds. Cut the pulp into slices.

Whip the cream and fold it into the cooled coconut milk mixture. Spoon it into the cooled tart shell.

Arrange the slices of fruit over the cream mixture, alternating pineapple and papaya, and decorate with shredded coconut.

BLACKCURRANT
AND BLACKBERRY CRUMBLE TART

Ingredients

½ cup (125 g) unsalted butter, softened
1 cup (100 g) flour
1 cup plus 3 tablespoons (100 g) ground almonds
½ cup (100 g) brown sugar
12 oz (350 g) raspberries
¼ cup (50 g) granulated sugar
8 oz (250 g) blackcurrants
8 oz (250 g) blackberries

Preparation time: 20 minutes
Baking time: 10 minutes
6 parfait glasses and 1 baking tray.

Preheat the oven to 350°F (170°C).

Cut up the butter. In a mixing bowl, work the flour, the ground almonds, the butter, and the brown sugar with your fingertips until the combination forms coarse crumbs. Line a baking tray with waxed paper and spread this mixture over it. Bake for 10 minutes.

Puree the raspberries and granulated sugar together to make a coulis.

Spoon some of the coulis into the bottom of the glasses, add the other berries, pour more coulis over them, and cover with crumble topping.

POACHED
PEACH TART

Ingredients

½ lb (250 g) almond shortbread pastry (see recipe p. 12)
1 ½ pints (750 ml) fruity red wine
¾ cup (150 g) granulated sugar
1 cinnamon stick
1 vanilla pod, slit lengthways
2 star anise
2 lb (1 kg) white peaches

Preparation time: 50 minutes
Baking time: 1 hour 15 minutes
**Baking pan: one 9-inch (24-cm) square
or one 10-inch (26-cm) round pan.**

Preheat the oven to 325°F (160°C).

Line the pan with the almond shortbread pastry. Pre-bake for 30 minutes (see p. 22). Remove from oven and leave to cool before unmolding.

Bring the wine to the boil in a saucepan. Lower the heat and add ½ cup (100 g) sugar, the cinnamon stick, the slit vanilla pod, and 2 star anise.

Peel the peaches, cut in half, and remove the pits. Set aside four halves. Place the rest in the boiling wine and simmer gently for 35 minutes.

Remove from heat, drain the peaches, and leave to cool. Cut the peaches into slices. Bring the wine to the boil again and reduce to a syrupy consistency.

In a saucepan, gently reduce the remaining four peach halves and the ¼ cup (50 g) sugar to a puree. Leave to cool.

Before serving, spread the peach puree over the crust. Arrange the peaches attractively and glaze with red wine syrup.

BRETON SHORTBREAD
WITH WILD STRAWBERRIES

Preparation time: 30 minutes
Baking time: 30 minutes
Baking pan: one 9-inch (24-cm) square
or one 10-inch (26-cm) round pan.

Ingredients

7 oz (200 g) Breton shortbread pastry (see recipe p. 12)
5 egg yolks
1 cup (250 ml) whole milk
¼ cup (50 g) granulated sugar
3 tablespoons (30 g) cornstarch
14 oz (400 g) wild strawberries or small, flavorful strawberries
Shredded coconut for decoration

Preheat the oven to 300°F (150°C).

Line the baking pan with the Breton shortbread pastry.

Dilute one egg yolk with a little water and brush the mixture over the shell. Bake for 30 minutes. In a saucepan, bring the milk to the boil. In a mixing bowl, beat the other 4 egg yolks together with the sugar and the cornstarch. Pour the hot milk over the mixture, beating all the time. Return the mixture to the saucepan and bring it back to a simmer, stirring all the time. Remove from heat and allow to cool.

Remove the baking pan from the oven and set aside to cool. Spread the custard mixture evenly over the crust and arrange the wild strawberries attractively on top.

 Garnish with shredded coconut.

TWO-GRAPE TART

Ingredients

½ lb (250 g) almond shortbread pastry (see recipe p. 12)
10 oz (300 g) red grapes
10 oz (300 g) white grapes
1 cup (250 ml) whole milk
2 egg yolks
¼ cup (50 g) granulated sugar
3 tablespoons (30 g) cornstarch
½ cup (100 g) heavy cream (30-40 percent butterfat) or crème fraîche

Preparation time: 30 minutes
Baking time: 30 minutes
Baking pan: one 9-inch (24-cm) square
or one 10-inch (26-cm) round pan.

Preheat the oven to 325°F (160°C).

Line the pan with the almond shortbread pastry. Pre-bake for 30 minutes (see p. 22) and set aside to cool.

Wash grapes, remove stalks, and dry them on paper towel.

In a saucepan, bring the milk to a boil.

In a mixing bowl, beat the egg yolks together with the sugar and the cornstarch. Pour the hot milk over the mixture, beating all the time. Pour the liquid back into the saucepan, and bring back to a simmer, beating constantly. Remove from heat, set aside to cool, and then chill in refrigerator.

Whip the cream and fold it carefully into the custard mixture.

Spread the cream mixture evenly into the cool tart shell.

Cut the grapes in half and arrange them attractively on the cream.

STRAWBERRIES ON FRENCH TOAST

Ingredients

1 ½ lb (700 g) strawberries
6 eggs
1 ½ pints (750 ml) whole milk
10 slices Kayser tourte bread or Kayser baguette
½ cup (100 g) brown sugar
1 ½ tablespoons (20 g) salted butter

Preparation time: 20 minutes
Baking time: 15 minutes
One ceramic ovenproof dish,
12 x 8 inches (20 cm x 30 cm).

Preheat the oven to 350°F (180°C).

Wash, hull, and dry the strawberries.

In a mixing bowl, beat the eggs.

In a saucepan, bring the milk to the boil.

Remove the crusts from the bread and very briefly soak the soft part in the hot milk. Then dip the bread in the beaten eggs.

Line the pan with the soaked bread, leaving no gaps between slices or around the edges. You will have to cut some of the bread so that it fits in exactly.

Sprinkle half the brown sugar over the bread and bake for 15 minutes. Remove the dish, and turn oven to broil function.

Cut the strawberries into slices, lengthways, and arrange them over the toasted bread. Sprinkle them with the remaining sugar, and dot with knobs of butter. Caramelize lightly under the broiler.

 Serve warm with vanilla ice cream.

MINTED
MELON TART

Ingredients

½ lb (250 g) almond shortbread pastry (see recipe p. 12)
1 cup (250 ml) whole milk
3 egg yolks
¼ cup (50 g) granulated sugar
¼ cup (25 g) flour
1 ½ tablespoons (15 g) cornstarch
2 large melons
1 bunch of fresh mint

Preparation time: 25 minutes
Baking time: 25 minutes
Baking pan: one 9-inch (24-cm) square
or one 10-inch (26-cm) round pan.

Heat the oven to 325°F (160°C).

Line the baking pan with the almond shortbread pastry. Pre-bake it for 25 minutes (see p. 22). Allow to cool.

In a saucepan, bring the milk to the boil. In a mixing bowl, beat the egg yolks together with the sugar, the flour, and the cornstarch. Pour a little of the hot milk into this mixture and beat together. Pour it back into the saucepan. Bring it up to the boil again, stirring constantly with a wooden spoon. Remove from the heat and set aside to cool.

Cut the melons in two, remove the seeds and, using a melon scoop, form small balls with the flesh. Set aside.

Use a knife to scrape the rest of the melon flesh from the skins. Puree it and spoon over the cooled pastry shell.

Spoon the cooled custard mixture into the shell. Gently arrange the melon scoops on the tart, and scatter chopped mint leaves to decorate.

APPLE
AND RAISIN TART

Ingredients

10 oz (300 g) puff pastry (see recipe p. 14)
1 cup (150 g) raisins
½ cup (100 ml) gold rum
1 ½ lb (600 g) apples
8 eggs
1 cup (200 g) granulated sugar
½ cup (50 g) flour
2 ¾ cups (400 g) heavy cream (30–40 percent butterfat) or crème fraîche
¾ teaspoon (4 g) vanilla extract
Confectioners' sugar for decoration

Preparation time: 30 minutes
Refrigeration time: 30 minutes
Baking time: 1 hour
1 9-inch (24 cm) cake pan.

Heat the oven to 300°F (150°C).

Heat the rum slightly. Plump the raisins in it for 30 minutes, then remove with a slotted spoon.

Line the baking pan with the puff pastry and refrigerate for 30 minutes.

Peel the apples and cut them in halves. Working from the skin, slit each half into several slices, without separating them.

In a mixing bowl, beat the eggs and the sugar together. Add the flour, the cream, and the vanilla extract. Mix thoroughly.

Tightly pack the apple halves into the pan. Scatter with raisins, and cover the fruit with the batter. Bake for 50 to 60 minutes.

 Allow to cool, and dust with confectioners' sugar.

LEMON TART

Ingredients

½ lb (250 g) shortbread pastry (see recipe p. 11)
4 unsprayed lemons
2 pints (1 liter) water
4 cups (750 g) granulated sugar
4 eggs
⅔ cup (160 ml) lemon juice
1 ⅓ cups (300 g) unsalted butter

Preparation time: 40 minutes
Baking time: 1 hour 10 minutes
Baking pan: one square 9-inch (24-cm)
or one round 10-inch (26-cm) pan.

Heat the oven to 325°F (160°C).

Wash and dry the lemons. Cut 3 lemons into thin slices. Finely grate the zest of the remaining lemon.

Bring 2 pints (1 liter) water to the boil together with 2 ½ cups (500 g) of the granulated sugar. Poach the lemon slices in the syrup for 10 minutes. Drain them and set aside.

Line the baking pan with the shortbread pastry. Pre-bake for 25 minutes (see p. 22).

In a mixing bowl, beat the eggs with 1 ¼ cup (250 g) granulated sugar. Add the lemon juice and zest. Pour the mixture into a bain-marie and cook, stirring constantly, until it starts to thicken (this should take about 45 minutes).

Remove from heat and mix in the butter. Spoon the mixture into the tart shell and leave to cool.

Decorate the tart with the poached lemon slices, arranging them so that they overlap slightly.

 Serve cool.

ERIC KAYSER

My Chocolate Tarts

The first chocolate tart I ever ate as a child was, quite simply, bread and chocolate: a thick slice of country bread, butter, sugar, and shavings of dark chocolate. To this day, it's still my favorite.

CHOCOLATE HAZELNUT TART

Ingredients

½ lb (250 g) almond shortbread pastry (see recipe p. 12)
2 cups (500 ml) whipping cream
7 oz (210 g) bittersweet chocolate (55 percent cocoa)
7 oz (210 g) milk chocolate
½ cup (100 g) unsalted butter
1 cup (200 g) granulated sugar
4 whole eggs
3 egg yolks
2 oz (60 g) toasted, chopped hazelnuts

Chocolate icing

3 ½ oz (100 g) bittersweet chocolate (55 percent cocoa)
⅔ cup (150 g) whipping cream

Preparation time: 35 minutes
Baking time: 30 minutes
Baking pan: one 9-inch (24-cm) square
or one 10-inch (26-cm) round pan.

Preheat the oven to 325°F (160°C). Line the baking pan with the almond shortbread pastry and pre-bake for 20 minutes (see p. 22).

In a saucepan, bring the cream to the boil. Break the bittersweet and milk chocolate into pieces. Remove the cream from the heat, and add the butter, the chocolate, and the sugar. Mix until all ingredients are thoroughly blended. Allow to cool down slightly, but it should still be warm for the next step.

Add the whole eggs, one by one, beating constantly, and then add the egg yolks, still beating. Pour the chocolate mixture into the tart shell and bake for 10 minutes.

Prepare the icing:
Break the chocolate into pieces. Heat the cream in a saucepan. Remove from heat and add the chocolate. Mix thoroughly.

Remove the tart from the oven and pour icing over. Allow to cool.

Scatter with toasted, chopped hazelnuts.

CHOCOLATE COCONUT TART

Preparation time: 15 minutes
Baking time: 35 minutes
Baking pan: one 9-inch (24 cm) square
or one 10-inch (26-cm) round pan.

Ingredients

½ lb (250 g) chocolate shortbread pastry (see recipe p. 13)
1 ¼ cup (300 ml) coconut milk
1 cup (200 g) whipping cream
1 lb (500 g) bittersweet chocolate (55 percent cocoa)
2 oz (70 g) shredded coconut, and a little more for decoration

Preheat the oven to 325°F (160°C).

Line the baking pan with the chocolate shortbread pastry and pre-bake for 35 minutes (see p. 22). Set aside to cool.

In a saucepan, heat the coconut milk and the whipping cream. Break the chocolate into pieces. Remove mixture from heat, add the chocolate, and mix thoroughly. Stir in the shredded coconut.

Fill the tart shell with the chocolate ganache and allow to cool. Sprinkle with shredded coconut.

MILK CHOCOLATE
AND CARAMEL TART

Ingredients

½ lb (250 g) chocolate shortbread pastry (see recipe p. 13)
1 ½ cups (300 g) granulated sugar
1 cup (250 g) heavy cream (30–40 percent butterfat) or crème fraîche
¼ cup (50 g) butter
2 whole eggs
1 egg yolk
2 ½ tablespoons (15 g) flour
1 ¼ cups (300 g) whipping cream
½ lb (250 g) milk chocolate

Preparation time: 40 minutes
Baking time: 30 minutes
Refrigeration time: 1 hour
One 9-inch (24-cm) square
or one 10-inch (26-cm) round baking pan.

Preheat the oven to 325°F (160°C).

Line the baking pan with the chocolate shortbread pastry and bake blind for 15 minutes (see p. 22).

In a saucepan, caramelize 1 cup (200 g) granulated sugar using the dry method until it turns a golden caramel color. Incorporate the heavy cream or crème fraîche and then add the butter. Mix thoroughly. Set aside to cool.

In a mixing bowl, beat the whole eggs with the extra egg yolk, then incorporate the flour.

Pour this into the cream-caramel mixture and mix thoroughly.

Spread it out in the tart shell and bake for 15 minutes. Remove from oven and allow to cool.

Prepare the milk chocolate mousse: beat the whipping cream until stiff. Melt the milk chocolate in the microwave or in a bain-marie, and fold it gently into the whipped cream.

Pour the chocolate mousse over the cooled caramel mixture, smoothing it with a spatula. Chill for one hour in the refrigerator.

To decorate: melt ½ cup (100 g) granulated sugar in a saucepan until it reaches an amber color. Pour it onto waxed paper laid out on a flat surface. Leave to cool. Break it into small fragments and stick them lightly into the top of the tart.

BITTERSWEET CHOCOLATE TART WITH PIMENT D'ESPELETTE

Preparation time: 10 minutes
Baking time: 35 minutes
Baking pan: one 9-inch (24-cm)
square or one 10-inch
(26-cm) round baking pan.

Ingredients

½ lb (250 g) chocolate shortbread pastry (see recipe p. 13)
1 ¼ cups (300 g) whipping cream
1 teaspoon ground piment d'Espelette (chili pepper from the Basque region),
    and a little more for decoration
14 oz (400 g) bittersweet chocolate
⅓ cup (70 g) butter

Preheat the oven to 325°F (160°C).

Line the baking pan with the chocolate shortbread pastry and pre-bake for 35 minutes (see p. 22). Set aside to cool. In a saucepan, heat the cream together with the piment d'Espelette.

Remove the cream from the heat. Break the chocolate into pieces and dissolve in the cream. Add the butter and mix through until quite dissolved.

Pour the chocolate ganache into the pastry shell. Allow to cool.

 Sprinkle with piment d'Espelette according to taste.

CHOCOLATE GINGERBREAD TART

Preparation time: 20 minutes
Baking time: 35 minutes
Baking pan: one 9-inch (24-cm)
square or one 10-inch
(26-cm) round baking pan.

Ingredients

½ lb (250 g) chocolate shortbread pastry (see recipe p. 13)
7 oz (200 g) gingerbread, and one slice for decoration
2 cups (500 ml) whole milk
12 oz (350 g) bittersweet chocolate, broken into small pieces

Preheat the oven to 325°F (160°C).

Line the baking pan with the chocolate shortbread pastry and bake blind for 35 minutes (see p. 22).

Remove the crusts from the gingerbread and cut the slices into small pieces.

Heat the milk in a saucepan and add the pieces of gingerbread. Mix until the pieces have completely disintegrated.

Remove from heat, add the bittersweet chocolate, and mix thoroughly.

Pour the mixture into the tart shell and allow to cool.

Toast the extra slice of gingerbread. Cut it into small, irregular pieces to decorate the tart.

CHOCOLATE TRIO

Ingredients

10 oz (300 g) chocolate shortbread pastry (see recipe p. 13)

Bittersweet chocolate ganache

1 cup (200 g) heavy cream (30–40 percent butterfat) or crème fraîche
8 oz (250 g) bittersweet chocolate
2 ½ tablespoons (35 g) unsalted butter

Milk chocolate ganache

1 cup (200 g) heavy cream (30–40 percent butterfat) or crème fraîche
10 oz (300 g) milk chocolate
1 ½ tablespoons (20 g) unsalted butter

White chocolate ganache

1 cup (200 g) heavy cream (30–40 percent butterfat) or crème fraîche
14 oz (400 g) white chocolate

To decorate

White chocolate shavings
Unsweetened cocoa powder

Preparation time: 40 minutes
Baking time: 30 minutes
Refrigeration time: 1 hour
Baking pan: one 9-inch (24-cm) square
or one 10-inch (26-cm) round pan.

Preheat the oven to 325°F (160°C).

Line the baking pan with the chocolate shortbread pastry and pre-bake for 30 minutes (see p. 22). Set aside to cool.

Prepare the three ganaches in the same way: Break the chocolate into pieces. In a saucepan, heat the cream and add the chocolate, mixing until it is melted. Remove from heat. Add butter to the bittersweet and milk chocolate ganaches. Mix thoroughly.

Pour the bittersweet ganache into the tart shell. Allow to cool. Pour the white chocolate ganache over this and allow to cool. Pour in the milk chocolate ganache. Allow to cool for 1 hour and then refrigerate.

 Decorate with chocolate shavings and sprinkle with cocoa powder.

CHOCOCRUMBLE TART

Ingredients
½ lb (250 g) chocolate shortbread pastry (see recipe p. 13)

Ganache
1 ⅔ cups (400 g) whipping cream
1 lb (500 g) bittersweet chocolate
⅓ cup (70 g) butter

Crumble topping
½ cup (100 g) unsalted butter
1 cup plus 3 tablespoons (100 g) ground almonds
½ cup (100 g) brown sugar
2 teaspoons (5 g) cocoa powder,
    unsweetened, and a little more for decoration

Preparation time: 30 minutes
Baking time: 40 minutes
Baking pan: one 9-inch (24-cm)
square or one 10-inch
(26-cm) round baking pan.

Preheat the oven to 325°F (160°C).

Line the baking pan with the chocolate shortbread pastry and pre-bake for 30 minutes (see p. 22).

Break the chocolate into small pieces. Heat the cream in a saucepan. Remove from heat and add chocolate. Mix thoroughly, then stir in the butter until the texture is smooth. Pour the ganache into the pastry shell and set aside to cool.

For the crumble: Dice the butter. In a mixing bowl, rub the ground almonds, the butter, the brown sugar, and the cocoa powder with your fingertips to form coarse crumbs. Line a baking tray with waxed paper. Spread the mixture over this and bake for 8 minutes. Remove and allow to cool.

 Spoon the crumble topping over the tart and sprinkle with cocoa powder.

FLAMBÉED BANANA CHOCOLATE TART

Preparation time: 20 minutes
Baking time: 25 minutes
Baking pan: one 9-inch (24-cm)
square or one 10-inch
(26-cm) round baking pan.

Ingredients

½ lb (250 g) chocolate shortbread pastry (see recipe p. 13)
3 oz (85 g) dark chocolate, minimum 70 percent cocoa solids
⅔ cup (150 g) butter
3 eggs
1 cup plus 2 tablespoons (220 g) granulated sugar
¾ cup (75 g) flour
3 bananas
1 ½ tablespoons (20 g) brown sugar
3 tablespoons (50 ml) gold rum

Preheat the oven to 325°F (160°C). Line the baking pan with the chocolate shortbread pastry.

Melt the chocolate together with the butter in a bain-marie or in the microwave.

In a mixing bowl, beat the eggs with the sugar. Sift in the flour and mix through.

Incorporate the melted chocolate and butter. Pour the mixture into the pastry shell.

Peel the bananas and cut them into slices. Arrange them over the chocolate mixture. Sprinkle the brown sugar on top and bake for 25 minutes.

Remove the tart from the oven. Heat the rum in a small saucepan, pour it over the tart, and flambé.

 Serve hot, warm, or cool.

ERIC KAYSER

My Sweet Tarts

You can do wonderful things with candies and crusts. Top your pastry with your favorite candy, dust your tarts with confectioners' sugar, or heap dollops of whipped cream on top, and let the sweetness work its magic.

SALTED
CARAMEL TART

Preparation time: 10 minutes
Baking time: 25 minutes
Baking pan: one 9-inch (24-cm)
square or one 10-inch
(26-cm) round baking pan.

Ingredients
7 oz (200 g) shortbread pastry (see recipe p. 11)
1 ½ cups (300 g) whipping cream
1 ½ cups (300 g) granulated sugar
⅔ cup (150 g) salted butter

Preheat the oven to 325°F (160°C).

Line the pan with the shortbread pastry and bake blind for 25 minutes (see p. 22).

In a saucepan, bring the cream to a boil.

Heat the sugar in another saucepan until it turns an amber color. Gradually pour in the hot cream, stirring constantly. Simmer for 5 minutes, continuing to stir.

Pour the caramel into the pastry shell and leave to cool.

MIXED DRIED FRUIT AND NUT TART

Ingredients for three tarts

2 lbs (1 kg) flour
1 ½ tablespoons (22 g) salt
1 tablespoon (20 g) yeast
½ cup (90 g) brown sugar
½ cup (50 g) powdered milk
1 pint (500 ml) water
⅔ cup (150 g) butter
3 ½ oz (100 g) raisins, soaked in rum
3 ½ oz (100 g) dried figs
3 ½ oz (100 g) whole unsalted almonds
3 ½ oz (100 g) pecan nuts
3 ½ oz (100 g) whole hazelnuts
3 ½ oz (100 g) candied orange peel, whole or cut into pieces
1 egg yolk

Preparation time: 25 minutes
Resting time: 1 hour 30 minutes
Baking time: 20 minutes
**To bake: 1 baking tray lined
with waxed paper.**

In a food processor bowl, mix the flour, salt, yeast, ⅓ cup of the brown sugar, powdered milk, and 1 pint (500 ml) water. Knead the mixture until elastic. Dice the butter, add to the dough, and knead again for 10 minutes.

Pour the mixture into a bowl and carefully and thoroughly fold in the fruit, nuts, and orange peel using a wooden spoon. Leave to rise in a warm place for 30 minutes.

Roll out the dough into a circle about 1 inch thick. Leave it to rise again for about 1 hour at room temperature. Preheat the oven to 350°F (170°C).

Add a little water to the egg yolk to brush on dough. Sprinkle with remaining brown sugar. Bake for 20 minutes.

 Serve warm or cool.

CHESTNUT TART

Preparation time: 40 minutes
Baking time: 30 minutes
Refrigeration time: 1 hour
Baking pan: one 9-inch (24-cm) square
or one 10-inch (26-cm) round pan.

Ingredients

½ lb (250 g) chocolate shortbread pastry (see recipe p. 13)
2 ½ sheets (4 g) leaf gelatin
2 oz (50 g) chestnut paste or chestnut purée
5 oz (140 g) chestnut cream
2 tablespoons (30 ml) gold rum
3 oz (80 g) glacéed chestnuts, chopped, plus a few for decoration
1 cup (245 g) cream (30 percent butterfat), or crème fraîche

Chocolate sauce

1 ¼ cups (300 g) whipping cream
5 oz (150 g) bittersweet chocolate

Preheat the oven to 325°F (160°C).

Line the pan with the chocolate shortbread pastry. Pre-bake for 30 minutes (see p. 22).

Leave the leaf gelatin to soften in a bowl of cold water.

In a mixing bowl, combine the chestnut paste or purée with the chestnut cream, the rum, and the chopped chestnuts.

Heat 2 ½ tablespoons (20 g) of the cream in a small saucepan. Remove the gelatin leaves from the water and squeeze out the excess water with your hands. Add the gelatin to the cream and mix until thoroughly dissolved. Pour this into the chestnut mixture and mix through.

Whip the remainder of the heavy cream and fold it delicately into the chestnut mixture until thoroughly incorporated.

Pour the chestnut mixture into the tart shell and refrigerate for 1 hour.

Break the chocolate into small pieces. In a saucepan, bring the whipping cream to the boil. Add chocolate. Stir until thoroughly mixed. Set aside to cool.

Pour the chocolate sauce over the chestnut tart and decorate with glacéed chestnuts.

PINK CARAMELIZED ALMOND TART

Preparation time: 20 minutes
Resting time: 1 hour
Baking time: 25 minutes
To bake: 1 baking tray
and waxed paper.

Ingredients

12 oz (350 g) brioche dough (see recipe p. 18)
1 cup (250 ml) whole milk
4 egg yolks
¼ cup (50 g) granulated sugar
3 tablespoons (30 g) cornstarch
7 oz (200 g) pink caramelized almonds

Cover the baking tray with the waxed paper. Roll out the brioche dough in a circle just under 1 inch thick and transfer to the baking tray.

In a saucepan, bring the milk to the boil.

In a mixing bowl, beat the egg yolks together with the sugar and the cornstarch. Pour the boiling milk over this and mix. Pour the batter back into the saucepan and bring to the boil again. Stir thoroughly, remove from the heat, and set aside to cool.

Pour the cooled mixture over the dough. Chop the caramelized almonds and sprinkle over the top.

Leave to rise for 1 hour at room temperature.

Preheat the oven to 325°F (160°C). Bake for 25 minutes.

FIG AND PECAN TART

Preparation time: 25 minutes
Baking time: 30 minutes
Baking pan: 9-inch (24-cm) square
or one 10-inch (26-cm)
round baking pan.

Ingredients

½ lb (250 g) shortbread pastry (see recipe p. 11)
½ cup (125 g) unsalted butter, softened
1 cup plus 3 tablespoons (225 g) granulated sugar
2 tablespoons (10 g) cake flour
1 ½ cups (125 g) ground almonds
2 teaspoons (10 ml) gold rum
3 eggs
5 oz (150 g) fresh figs
4 oz (125 g) pecans

Preheat the oven to 300°F (150°C).

Line the baking pan with the shortbread pastry.

Cream the butter in a mixing bowl. Add ⅔ cup (125 g) granulated sugar, flour, ground almonds, and rum. Mix until smooth. Add the eggs, one by one, beating rapidly all the time.

Wash the figs and cut them each into 8 pieces.

Pour half the batter into the pastry shell. Arrange half the figs and half the pecans over this. Cover with the rest of the mixture and bake for 30 minutes.

In a nonstick skillet, caramelize the remaining ½ cup (100 g) sugar until it turns an amber color. Using a fork, roll the remaining pecans in the caramel. Remove them one by one and set aside to cool on waxed paper.

When the caramelized pecans have cooled, arrange them on top of the tart and serve.

Thanks

Eric Kayser expresses his warm thanks to the entire team who helped to create this book:
Brigitte Namour, whose idea it was;
Franck Colombié, pastry chef;
Alain Baudet and Yaïr Yosefi, chefs, who each lent a willing, talented, and enthusiastic hand;
Christian Larit, for his fine pictures;
and to all our trustworthy suppliers, as well as Flammarion.

Eric Kayser dedicates this book to the people who instilled in him two essential values:
Patrick Castagna, for being unfailingly demanding;
his father, Jean-Claude Kayser, for being unfailingly rigorous.

Thanks also to those who lent the crockery and accessories:
Luminarc
Guy Degrenne
Studio Nova
Sabre
Geneviève Lethu

Some photos were taken at the Eric Kayser bakery and restaurant, 85, Boulevard Malesherbes, Paris 8ᵉ, France.